A BODY OF WRITING

1990–1999

A Body of Writing
1990–1999

Bronwyn Davies

ALTAMIRA
PRESS

A Division of Rowman & Littlefield Publishers, Inc.
Walnut Creek • Lanham • New York • Oxford

For information contact:
AltaMira Press
A Division of Rowman & Littlefield Publishers, Inc.
1630 North Main Street, Suite 367
Walnut Creek, CA 94596
http://www.altamirapress.com

Rowman & Littlefield Publishers, Inc.
12 Hid's Copse Road
Cumnor Hill
Oxford OX2 9JJ, England

4720 Boston Way
Lanham, MD 20706

YUB

LD7

Copy 2

LANCASTER UNIVERSITY
-5 FEB 2004
LIBRARY

Library of Congress Cataloging-in-Publication Data
Davies, Bronwyn, 1945–
   A body of writing, 1990–1999 / Bronwyn Davies
     p. cm.
   Includes bibliographical references and data.
   Contents: Coming to writing—The process of subjectification—The problem of desire—The concept of agency—Women's subjectivity and feminist stories—Positioning: the discursive production of selves/with Rom Harré—Classroom competencies and marginal positionings/with Robyn Hunt—The subject of poststructuralism—Poststructuralist theory in practice: working with "behaviorally disturbed" children/with Cath Laws.
   ISBN 0-7425-0321-6 (cloth: alk. paper) — ISBN 0-7425-0322-4 (paper: alk. paper)
   1. Deconstruction. 2. Feminism and literature. I. Title.
PN98.D43 D38 2000
149—dc21   99-053859

Editorial Management: Jennifer R. Collier
Interior Design and Production: Rachel Fudge
Cover Design: Joanna Ebenstein

~ Contents

~ Acknowledgments

I WOULD LIKE TO THANK the co-authors of three of the chapters, Rom Harré, Robyn Hunt, and Cath Laws, for their generous permission to publish their work here and for the time spent with them in the pleasurable exchange of ideas, especially during the writing of these papers. There are many other people to whom I am intellectually indebted—people whose work I have read, people with whom I have talked, people who have hospitably taken care of me in my travels. It would not be possible to trace out the webs of conversational meaning-making that lead finally to the insights that eventually appear on the screen and then the page, though it is clear that none of these ideas could have emerged without such conversations. To all those people with whom I have had engaging conversations over the last decade, to my friends and my students, I offer my thanks. I would also like to thank Kirsten Gomard and Anne-Mette Kruse for their wonderful hospitality and friendship during my time at Cekvina, at the University of Århus, where I worked on this manuscript. I would like to thank Bronwyn Houldsworth and Rachel Fudge for their work on the manuscript, and also I would like to thank Jennifer Collier, my editor at AltaMira Press, who extended me her support and good advice during this project. To all the others I have not named but with whom I have had many pleasurable and productive conversations, I extend my thanks. I would also like to thank Hampton Press, Sage Publications, *Social Problems, Social Analysis, Journal for the Theory of Social Behavior, British Journal of Sociology of Education, Gender and Education,* and *International Journal of Qualitative Studies in Education* for their permission to publish the articles and chapters that have previously been published with them.

1 ~ Coming to writing

T HIS IS A "BODY OF WRITING" that brings together the ideas I was working on (and that were working on me) during the last decade. In this body
of writing I explore the language of poststructuralism with two agendas in
mind. The first is to make it accessible, understandable, and usable as a conceptual framework for interpreting and analyzing the social world. The second is to enter into its terms to find what life becomes when it is taken up
as a discourse of one's own. As Søndergaard (1999, p. 1) says, one has to
thoroughly "digest" the ideas of poststructuralist thought and to work in
quite complex ways to make them usable in the social sciences:

> [I]n its completely abstract form, post-structuralist thought is of virtually no
> empirical use. Post-structuralist ideas have first to be thoroughly digested prior to
> the construction of analytical tools. And all this has to take place in interaction
> with the field of enquiry to which the study is directed. We cannot simply carry
> post-structuralist ideas logically through a predetermined chain of reflections and
> hence arrive at a number of quite specific and inevitable analytic consequences.

Poststructuralist theories make visible the shifts not only in interpretation,
but also in the living of life that come about with the taking up of a new discourse. What can be said and understood and done using a poststructuralist
framework changes not only the nature of the research, but the nature of
understanding brought to the detail of everyday life—that detail in turn feed-
ing into an understanding of poststructuralist theories as they are used to
analyze the episodes of social life on which we cast our analytic gaze. At the
same time, because of the reflexive nature of poststructuralist thought, the
new modes of interpretation and of life lived in and through poststructuralist
discourses can never be finally accomplished. Poststructuralist thought does
not have a stable foundation that can ever be grasped once and for all. Its own
conceptual apparatus is always open to examination, not with questions such
as which concepts should be included or excluded, but rather: what work do
these concepts achieve; what can they make visible and what do they occlude;
who is given authority through their usage and who is deprived of it? Basic
to working with poststructuralist theories is recognizing oneself as discursively constituted and at the same time, as a poststructuralist writer, pushing
at the boundaries of one's own subjection. One explores the limits of subjectivity in order to find the ways of moving beyond those limits:

> For the individual, freedom from normalizing forms of individuality consists in an exploration of the limits of subjectivity. By interrogating what are held to be necessary boundaries to identity or the limits of subjectivity, the possibility of transgressing these boundaries is established and, therefore, the potential of creating new types of subjective experience is opened up. (McNay, 1994, pp. 145–46)

Poststructuralist theories provide conceptual possibilities that enable us to turn our gaze differently on the social world as it folds and unfolds around us; they also invite us to turn our analytic gaze on the ongoing processes of our own subjectification. As Deleuze says, when people are fascinated by Foucault "it's because they're doing something with him, in their own work, in their own independent lives. It's not just a question of intellectual understanding or agreement, but of intensity, resonance, musical harmony" (Deleuze, 1995, p. 86). In this book you will find intensities, resonances, and harmonies as I explore, sometimes with others, sometimes alone, the possible music that I can play with poststructuralist theories as I work with them to unfold the insights they can bring to human life.

Cixous has been a profound influence in my take-up of poststructuralist theory. Others, such as Valerie Walkerdine and Wendy Hollway, have used psychoanalytic theory as a way of incorporating individual subjectivities into their poststructuralist theorizing. My preference has been to draw on the writing of Hélène Cixous, who rejects psychoanalysis but draws on the detail of her own subjectivity, her own experience of living and of writing, to find the detailed ways both to understand the complex detail of subjection and to creatively move beyond some aspects of it. Cixous says in a conversation with Mireille Calle-Gruber (1997, p. 30):

> We live, but why do we live? I think: to become more human: more capable of reading the world, more capable of playing it in all ways. This does not mean nicer or more humanistic. I would say: more faithful to what we are made from and to what we can create.

The inclusion of my embodied self in this body of writing is not in order to produce an autobiographical account of a particular life (though of course it can be read that way), but because the detail of the texts of life as I have lived it as an embodied being provide an immediate and vivid resource for examining the constitutive power of discourse both as I find myself constituted and as I, in turn, constitute the world in my reading and writing of it. It is in examining one's own subjective take-up of the tangled threads of life that the most convincing evidence can be found for the arguments that poststructuralist theories make against universal explanatory schemas and false unities. "The interpretation of events according to a unifying totality deprives them of the impact of their own singularity and immediacy" (McNay, 1992, p. 13). And as Foucault (1984, p. 62) wrote:

> The world we know is not this ultimately simple configuration where events are reduced to accentuate their essential traits, their final meaning, or their initial and final value. On the contrary, it is a profusion of entangled events.

At the same time, it is, according to Butler (1995, p. 39), the capacity of poststructurally informed analyses to make the constitutive force of discourse visible that provides "the very precondition of a politically engaged critique." Not only do they provide the grounds for such critique, they provide the possible grounds for social and political movement. Because they do not seek to lock the reader/writer into false certainties, because they require an openness to understanding the effects of their own languages, their own activity, and because they require of the reader/writer an engaged, embodied understanding of what they *do,* poststructuralist theories are capable of making transformations visible. And in being open to the factors of instability and uncertainty one is also open to movement, to the passage from one state to another:

> [If] one remains open and susceptible to all the phenomena of overflowing, beginning with natural phenomena, one discovers the immense landscape of the *trans-,* of the passage. Which does not mean that everything will be adrift: our thinking, our choices etc. But it means that the factor of instability, the factor of uncertainty, or what Derrida calls the undecidable, is indissociable from human life. (Cixous, in Cixous and Calle-Gruber, 1997, p. 52)

There is a multidirectional force in poststructuralist thinking, one that insists on a faithful attention to the discursive detail that we are made from, and, in that very attention to the detail, an opening up to the multiple movements that we are capable of. I would like to think of this body of writing as containing just this multidirectional force.

The theoretical writing you find here takes as background and also as resource the various books I have written on gender and on schooling in which I have used a poststructuralist framework. I will therefore sketch out briefly what those books are about.

The first book that I wrote using a poststructuralist framework was *Frogs and Snails and Feminist Tales: Preschool Children and Gender,* published in 1989. I undertook this study because I had, in my own life, become fascinated by the way in which gender was, on occasion, made relevant when I had supposed it, in that context, to be completely irrelevant, such as in decisions about whether or not I was to become a tenured academic. I wanted to know how it was that gender came to matter so much to people, how it came to carry so much emotional weight and to shape perceptions and decision making to the extent that it did. It also seemed to me, as the mother of three children, that much of the theorizing about children and about the origins of gender was being done by people who'd never actually spent time with children, observing them and listening to them. I wanted to get as close as I could to the origins of the take-up of gendered being. To do that, I believed I needed to be able to talk to and listen to the gendered beings I was studying. Four- and five-year-old children seemed the obvious choice of people to work with. I read stories to them—in particular, feminist stories—and listened to the sense they made of them; I observed them in their play and questioned them about the meanings they were making; and at times I got caught up in their play and found myself emotionally flung back to the age of four and to the gendered power struggles being played out there.

At the same time as I was gathering the data from preschools in Australia, authors such as Valerie Walkerdine and Chris Weedon in the U.K. were publishing material that made poststructuralist theories both readable and usable. Chris Weedon showed in her book *Feminist Practice and Poststructuralist Theory* that poststructuralist theories could be made meaningful and usable by feminist activists. Valer̄ ̄̄̄ ̄̄ ̄̄̄ ̄̄ ̄̄̄ ̄̄ ̄ showed in her articles published in 1981, 1985, and 1987, for example, how the ideas being generated by poststructuralist theorists could be made relevant in the study of everyday situations in which gender or class was being constituted. I was fortunate to discover poststructuralist theories primarily through the writing of these two authors, as their ability to translate poststructuralist theorizing into a politics of action and into interpretive tools for social research turns out to be quite rare.

As I began interacting with the material I had gathered in my preschool study, it became readily obvious that I would be doing a terrible violence to it to interpret it in terms of well-known, well-used explanatory frameworks such as sex role socialization theory. Something much more dynamic and interesting was going on in my data that poststructuralist concepts made both visible and analyzable. When I came to the end of the preschool study, it was clear that the take-up of gender was so intricately woven out of and through the discursive practices available to children that its take-up in oppositional hierarchical terms was almost inevitable. Yet I was sure that that inevitability could be disrupted, or at least troubled a little, if only the discursive practices and their constitutive force were made visible. I decided to work with primary school children to see whether it was possible to enable them to see discourse and its constitutive force, and to interrupt the inevitability of their take-up of gender in the limited and limiting terms of the male/female dualism. At the same time, I wanted to provide the children with the discursive practices through which alternatives could be tried. That exploration is written up as *Shards of Glass: Children Reading and Writing Beyond Gendered Identities* (Davies, 1993).

One of the things that became clear in researching and writing *Shards of Glass* is how extraordinarily difficult it is for teachers to break old patterns of adult-child interaction. While it might be possible for me to imagine a troubling of old authoritative patterns and the introduction of new possibilities for thinking and being, old patterns of authority and knowledge seemed to reassert themselves outside the range of conscious attention of the various teachers with whom I was working. Reflexive awareness of one's own patterns of speaking and interacting in the very moment of interacting and speaking seemed to me not so difficult. But the capacity to become reflexively and critically literate, to catch oneself in the act of constituting the world in particular ways, seems, to most teachers I have talked to and worked with, outside the range of possibility. They asked me for recipe knowledges and practices that they could use without developing their own reflexive analytic strategies. Such recipe knowledges are incompatible with a poststructuralist approach—and so I have struggled on, examining my own and others' practices, working with teachers, giving them access to poststructuralist theorizing, helping them find ways to make their own practices visible and revisable. Two books, *Poststructuralist Theory and Classroom Practice* (Davies, 1994) and *Power, Knowledge, Desire: Changing School Organisation and Management Practices* (Davies, 1996a), are the result of this work. In these books I show what poststructurally informed teaching and practice might look like. I write from the perspective of teachers who are struggling to become aware of their own practices and to turn their own analytic gaze on their teaching contexts. What is interesting about this work, in the context of the theoretical writing gathered together in this book, is the certainty I had that poststructuralist thought was of immediate relevance to life lived and practiced. I did not imagine it as some discourse floating free of practice, nor as the discursive resource for a clever intellectual game to be played solely within the walls of academe. When others describe poststructuralist thought in these terms I find myself bemused and puzzled (Davies, 1998).

In each of these studies I collected data through observation, interviews, conversations, explorations of reading and writing against the grain of dominant discourses, and collaborative writing. At the same time, I drew on my own and others' lived history of being in the world whenever it seemed to cast light on the questions I was exploring. And I have used another, less well known strategy, which I have increasingly found useful in making poststructuralist concepts come to life in working with students and in finding answers to the questions I have been pursuing. This is Haug et al.'s (1987) strategy of collective memory work, a research technique particularly suited to poststructuralist theorizing because it begins with the particular memories of individual people—memories that they take to be their own personal stories, that belong to them, are of them, and that signify who they are—

their subjectivity. In the first telling of their story, related to the topic the group is working on, each of the participants imagine that their story will have little or no relation to the experiences of others. They expect their story to be understandable, but that its primary relevance is to mark them as separate and different. Through telling their stories and listening to each other's stories, and through careful questioning of each other's stories, each member of the group begins to recognize the ways in which their particular stories are *cultural* productions that intersect and overlap with the stories of others. Others' stories bear unexpected similarities to their own—and they engender a more detailed recall of their own stories. In particular, when others' stories appear to be opposite to one's own, each person begins to retrieve the contradictory elements in their own stories, to remember them not as linear and straightforward, reduced through explanation, but with all the complex, tangled detail of lived experience. Through an examination of the ways in which they have each taken up discourses as their own, at the same time and through the same processes through which they were subjected, the participants in a collective biography can come to reveal something of the tangled threads of life in its simultaneous shaping and constraining and opening up of possibilities for resistance. Haug et al. (1987, p. 60) say of this technique:

> If we are to outline strategies for liberation within patterns of thought drilled into us by others, then it seems to us essential to record the mental traces of those traditional patterns, to make conscious the ways in which we have hitherto unconsciously interpreted the world, and to develop resistances against this "normality". Only then will it become possible for us to identify the points at which our morality hinders the development of our thinking, the points at which images from the past reassert their hold on us in the present; the feelings we live in productions of our own.

The body of writing: a summary

In Chapter 2, "The process of subjectification," I explore how it is that we become seamlessly meshed in the social fabric, and yet know and signal ourselves as beings with specificity. This dual aspect of subjectification I see as the most difficult and important aspect of poststructuralist theory. Deleuze and Guattari (1987, p. 159) write: "You will be organized, you will be an organism, you will articulate your body. . . . You will be signifier and signified, interpreter and interpreted. . . . You will be a subject, nailed down as one, a subject of the enunciation recoiled into a subject of the statement." We are simultaneously constituted through discourse, "nailed down," "recoiling" into the text, and yet we become at the same time and through those same processes a speaking

Chapter 8, "The subject of poststructuralism," is a reply to a rather star-tling attack on my writing in which it was claimed that I was not, after all, authorized to speak and write poststructurally, since humanism could be found lurking in the words of the texts I had written. My use of words such as "choice" and "agency" were taken as evidence that I had imported the dreaded "humanist subject" into my texts, thus invalidating any claim I might make to be one who uses poststructuralist theorizing as it is meant to be used. Butler's theorizing is recommended to the reader as a preferable alternative to my writing, since it is more pure in its achievement of good poststructuralism in which the humanist subject cannot be found lurking. Butler (1995, p. 48) writes, as if responding in my defense:

> There is, of course, talk about the death of the subject, but *which* subject is that? And what is the status of the utterance that announces its passing? What speaks now that the subject is dead? That there is a speaking seems clear, for how else could the utterance be heard? So clearly, the death of that subject is not the death of agency, of speech, or of political debate.

I include only part of my reply to the attack on my work because much of the reply is a detailed critique of the attack itself, which is of no interest without that original text to hand. I found writing the reply rather an enjoy-able process, as it caused me to revisit and examine the discursive ground I'd been treading and to spell out more clearly some of the issues raised by the attack. This writing circles back to subjectification, to agency, and to posi-tioning, and it discusses their location in a poststructuralist framework. It explores what it means to be a subject and offers the idea of the subject as verb rather than noun, and of "selving" rather than "selves," signaling a rather Deleuzian turn in my thinking: "Bodies are not defined by their genus or species, by their organs and functions, but by what they can do, by the affects of which they are capable" (Deleuze and Parnet, 1987, p. 60). A body is anything that affects or is affected: "it can be animal, a body of sounds, a mind or an idea" (Deleuze, 1992, p. 629).

The final chapter, "Poststructuralist theory in practice," written with Cath Laws, is the culmination of these theoretical writings. It takes as its topic the positioning of some students as powerless, and it examines the ways in which a poststructurally informed school principal/researcher can work differently with those students, finding ways to unlock the inevitabil-ity of their positioning, but seeing at the same time the enormous constitu-tive power of the discursive practices through which their selves are ongoingly being constituted. This writing reveals the power of poststruc-turalist theorizing as a resource for understanding and guiding change, and as a means of understanding the enormous resistance to change that politically motivated researchers inevitably find themselves working with and against.

Notes on power

Through all of this writing the concept of power is used, but not defined anywhere. I have hesitated to attempt to pin it down because it is at once so elusive and so ubiquitous. Foucault writes about power as inextricable from knowledge, claiming that knowledge *is* power:

> For Nietzsche and Foucault the "is" connecting knowledge and power does not indicate that the relation of knowledge and power is one of predication such that knowledge leads to power. Rather, the relation is such that knowledge is not gained prior to and independently of the use to which it will be put in order to achieve power (whether over nature or other people), but is already a function of human interests and power relations. (Couzens Hoy, 1986, p. 129)

There are two ways in which the coalescence of knowledge and power appears in what I write about: that power resides first in what is taken to be knowledge, and second in the ways in which that which is taken to be known is framed in language. That which is taken as given, as either authoritatively so or less visibly so, as the way the world is taken for granted as being, shapes the possible actions and ways of being that we can imaginably engage in.

We cannot exist without being subjected through knowledge/discourse, and some of the systems of knowledge through which we are subjected are oppressive to some and give positions of advantage to others. At the same time, as we are necessarily and inevitably subjected by knowledge/discourse, power/knowledge can be thought of in terms of particular knowledges giving rise to the possibility of powerful action, either on the part of individuals or collectives. Thus power over other people may, in a sense, rest in the knowledge itself (in its particular constitutive effects), as well as in particular individual's or collective's uses of it. According to Couzens Hoy (1986, p. 134):

> Foucault wants to describe how power is *exercised*, and he sees that there would be no power if it were not exercised by agents. Foucault even uses the term "exercise of power" frequently, as in the title of his essay, "How is power exercised?" There he says explicitly that power is exercised by individuals or groups of individuals.

Power is not a thing or an essence that can be described, but a complex set of relations amongst people and in the relations between people and knowledge systems—or patterns of discourse. Along with Nietzsche and Foucault I see power not just as oppressive relations amongst people, and not solely restrictive in its effects. Power is also the power to do things, to resist, to deconstruct, to write, to create, to imagine, to laugh, to move people to tears, to experience *jouissance*. Power, in its more obvious and political and bureaucratic manifestations, is experienced by some who occupy subject positions that are defined as powerful. Once positioned as someone with the right to make decisions that affect other's lives, and to mobilize discourses that have powerful effects, individuals will find themselves, at least from time to time and within some situations, experiencing a sense of their own power to affect others with or without their consent. There is nothing guaranteed about such positioning, since there is no guarantee that all people will see the occupation of the subject position as legitimate, and there is no guarantee that anyone will continue to do so indefinitely. Nor is it inevitable that a person so positioned will use their positioning in oppressive or dominating ways, though it is highly likely that they will do so at least some of the time.

While I would not want to argue that power is in any sense possessed by or essential to individual persons who take up powerful subject positions and are positioned by others as legitimately doing so, I would want to recognize that some have privileged access to practicing, and so coming to embody, powerful ways of speaking and moving and interacting. Foucault observed that bodies are shaped and disciplined through the systemic pattern of power in our society, which "reaches into the very grain of individuals, touches their bodies and inserts itself into their actions and attitudes, their discourses, learning processes and everyday lives" (Foucault, 1980, p. 39). Privileged access to embodied power should not be thought of just in terms of class privilege and oppressive powers. Individuals and groups occasionally gain access to discourses and discursive practices that they are able to mobilize with very beneficial effects on a wide range of people. The two co-authors of chapters about aspects of schooling in this body of writing are examples of such embodied power, which is both practiced and habitual, and at the same time are restlessly searching for discourses that enable them to use that positioned and embodied power to enable others, who do not normally experience any form of power that is recognized as legitimate, to experience power in ways that are constituted as legitimate.

Harré's claim in *Social Being* (1979) that power is *no more than* a dramatic fiction can be misleading. Power is undoubtedly a dramatic fiction that nonetheless works in the lives of individuals and collectives, with powerful effects. To the extent that all social life can be understood as "fictional" (the result of discursive practices and shaped within the storylines of the culture), then it is not saying a great deal to call anything "merely fictional." The merely fictional is the fabric out of which real lives are lived and in which the effects of power and powerlessness can have devastating effects.

So at the same time as one might assent to the definition of power as a dramatic fiction, one would also want to argue that it is also an important term for drawing attention to, describing, and analyzing structural imbalances and patterns of practice that rob some subjects, and some groups of subjects, of the capacity to act in ways that will be recognized as legitimate by those who have been granted authority over the situations in which those robbed of legitimacy find themselves.

The desire for power in its most brutish manifestations leads to one group of people burning another at the stake (for having different ideas), or to committing mass genocide (of those who have different cultural practices, or who occupy desired space). In its less visible forms the desire for power may not be defined as such by those who, for example, systematically control and shape the lives of others who are seen as lacking in the discourses and practices of the dominant group. They may define their own actions, instead, as laudable, as "correcting" or "saving" another group from its own practices. They may remain oblivious to the fact that their activity is part of a complex system of ensuring that their own discourses and practices prevail as recognizably "superior," that recognized "superiority" facilitating their take-up of powerful positionings within the culture, and ensuring that their own utterances remain hearable as legitimate.

The unquestioning acceptance of discourses and practices that judge and find lacking those who have not had access to or who have been excluded from access to, or who do not desire access to, dominant discourses is a particular form of power that its wielders are often sadly unconscious of. As Couzens Hoy (1986, p. 142) observes:

> We experience power only in diverse and multiple ways at the "micro-level" when we find ourselves subjected to particular exercises of power (or more rarely, and perhaps without understanding our own facility or authority, when we exercise power over others).

Two of the chapters in this body of writing in particular, "Classroom competencies" and "Poststructuralist theory in practice," set out to analyze the tangled threads of the patterns of practice and discourse through which such oppressive patterns of power and powerlessness are constituted—and also how they might be resisted. In particular each paper examines the micro-level of the exercises of power to which Couzens Hoy refers.

2 ~ The process of subjectification

> Well I thought I'd never giggle again
>   to tell you the truth
> I felt really bad
> sitting like this on the bench in the playground
> after a minute you get totally bored
> and wish you were with your friends
>   smiling
>   We started laughing so much
>   we just couldn't stop
>   We just couldn't stop and
>   Mrs Brown told us to "shut up"
>   it was just so funny
> I always feel so different
>   from everyone else
> —*Jennifer, Eastern Public*

CHILDHOOD IS A TIME THAT IS DIFFICULT TO CAPTURE, so rich is it in new associations, emergent senses, connections, formings and unformings. As Virginia Woolf (1976, p. 93) says in her own memoirs of childhood:

> [T]he consciousness of other groups impinging upon ourselves; public opinion; what other people say and think; all those magnets which attract us this way to be like that, or repel us the other and make us different from that . . .
> . . . the "subject of this memoir" is tugged this way and that every day of his life; it is they that keep him in position. . . . I see myself as a fish in a stream; deflected; held in place; but cannot describe the stream.

A central tension in childhood as it is experienced in the modern world comes from the simultaneous struggles to be seamlessly meshed in the social fabric and to know and to signal oneself as a being with specificity. One's being must be able to be disattended by oneself and others, and at the same time be able to be identified as an individual, distinguishable from the rest. Further, that individual must have continuity of being and responsibility for

This chapter is taken in part from Chapter 2 of my book *Shards of Glass: Children Reading and Writing Beyond Gendered Identity,* published by Allen and Unwin and Hampton Press in 1993.

his or her actions. One of the primary means for achieving this continuity is through story:

> We live immersed in narrative, recounting and reassessing the meaning of our past actions, anticipating the outcomes of our future projects, situating ourselves at the intersections of several stories not yet completed. (Brooks, 1984, p. 3)

Each child must locate and take up as their own narratives of themselves that knit together the details of their existence. At the same time they must learn to be coherent members of others' narratives. Through stories we each constitute ourselves and each other as beings with specificity. Benhabib defines the achievement of self as "how I, as a finite, concrete, embodied individual, shape and fashion the circumstances of my birth and family, linguistic, cultural and gender identity into a coherent narrative that stands as my life's story" (1987, p. 166). Porter adds to this: "A narrative approach has two inseparable components. That is, *I am the subject of a history* with a particular personal meaning, and *I am part of others' stories*" (1991, p. 20).

In order to achieve these narratives of oneself and others, children must learn the ways of seeing made possible by the various discursive practices of the social groups of which they are members. This is not simply a cognitive process of language learning, but also an ability to read and interpret the landscape of the social world, and to embody, to live, to experience, to know, to desire *as one's own*, to take pleasure in the world, as it is made knowable through the available practices, and in particular the discursive practices, the patterns of power and powerlessness and one's positioning within them. Correct membership of the social order entails being able to read situations correctly such that what is obvious to everyone else is also obvious to you. It involves knowing how to be positioned and to position oneself as a member of the group who knows and takes for granted what other people know and take for granted in a number of different settings. Althusser uses the term *obviousness* to capture this taken-for-granted quality of the discursive categories, and in particular of the ways of being a "subject," through which we construct our lives:

> [I]t is clear that you and I are subjects (free, ethical, etc.). Like all obviousnesses, including those that make a word "name a thing" or "have meaning" (therefore including the obviousness of the transparency of language), the "obviousness" that you and I are subjects—and that does not cause any problems—is an ideological effect, the elementary ideological effect. It is indeed a peculiarity of ideology that it imposes (without appearing to do so, since these are "obviousnesses") obviousnesses as obviousnesses, which we cannot *fail to*

recognize and before which we have the inevitable and natural reaction of cry-ing out (aloud or in the "still small voice of conscience"): "That's obvious! That's right! That's true!" (Althusser, 1984, pp. 45–46)

Each person in a social group both shares a set of obviousnesses and is positioned in relation to them—the nature of the positioning depending in large part on the individual's perceived category memberships. Those cate-gory memberships are most often conceptually and practically elements of an oppositional binary pair. So, for example, someone positioned as child (and therefore not adult), as student (and therefore not teacher), or as girl (and therefore not boy) must make these obviousnesses their own from each of these binary positionings. They must do this both as they make sense from within the categories in which they are positioned *and* from the position of its binary opposite, seeing themselves, not just from the inside of their assigned category looking out, but also from the position of their binary opposite.

In *Frogs and Snails* (Davies, 1989a) I developed the idea of category main-tenance work, whereby children ensure that the categories of person, as they are coming to understand them, are maintained as meaningful categories in their own actions and the actions of those around them. In Althusser's terms, the children in that study were asserting the obviousness of those cat-egories by signaling the unacceptability of activities that disrupt and the obvious meaning of the categories (that meaning that "we cannot fail to rec-ognize"). In particular I observed them engaging in category maintenance work around any activities that disrupted the obviousness that each of them was exclusively male or female. Male and female were achieved in this activ-ity as opposite categories that take their meaning in a hierarchical relation to each other.

Social competence is thus fundamentally to do with appearing as normal or "unpassremarkable" within the terms of the available, apparently trans-parent categories. An ability to appear in this way requires the sharing of a set of obviousnesses. Sometimes the features that disrupt this appearance are outside of the control of the child.

Vulnerability to isolation and to teasing (the naming by others of one-self as inappropriate) if one does not achieve social competence as it is defined by those others is a readily observable aspect of life in primary school (Davies, 1982). That teasing is most usually understood as "peer pressure" by which the group chooses to make the individual conform to a more or less arbitrary set of "norms." But it can be better understood as the struggle of the group individually and collectively to achieve themselves as knowable individuals within a predictable, knowable, transparent collec-tive reality.

In *Shards of Glass* (Davies, 1993) I analyze the work that Chas Banks undertook with several groups of primary school children. In that work, she and I were exploring ways to make visible to the children the patterns of power and powerlessness and the multiple and conflicting discourses through which gender is accomplished as an obvious and taken-for-granted fact of everyday life. We were setting out to disrupt the obviousness and thus the inevitability of the patterns of power and powerlessness in which they were caught up.

The conversation with Jennifer with which this chapter began took place in a one-to-one discussion with Chas. They were looking at the photos that Jennifer had taken as part of our project. This conversation readily makes visible the power she attributes to others in her struggle to inhabit the subject position of "friend" as she is positioned and positions herself within it. There is a tension between her access to specificity, with its attendant right to be different, and her access to group membership, which assumes and achieves sameness. There is at the same time a struggle to achieve the perceived requirement of a continuous and unitary self. She describes herself as usually cheerful and caught up in a pattern of expectations that she will always be so. Her explanations for this are that she is relatively new to the school, having come from New Zealand. She is different from the others in that they have better clothes and are slimmer than she is. She wishes her friends would recognize and accept her specificity and her variability as a being who is not always happy. She is intensely aware of moments of fear and unhappiness: "I thought I'd never giggle again, to tell you the truth." Her friends, in contrast, appear to her to be persons whose specificity and variability can be acknowledged in this way. But because she fears being caught up in the storyline in which moody people are isolated, left with no position to occupy except as marginal outsiders, she shrinks from having her own moods recognized. The anxieties she experiences about how she is spoken into existence by her friends cannot be revealed to them because of the possibility that she will be marginalized, made peripheral to the group. Thus when Jennifer turns her reflective gaze on herself, she refuses herself permission to take the freedoms that she sees her friends taking, for fear of becoming not one of them:

Jennifer: At school, you know, I've sort of got to be happy to everyone at school, 'cause I'm still really a newcomer. Well not a newcomer anymore but if I sort of show me being moody they um they sort of don't like me anymore. They can't stand me being moody, 'cause they can get moody but I can't. . . .

Well, I thought I'd never giggle again, to tell you the truth. . . . You know, this morning I felt really bad, yesterday I felt really bad and then me and Stacey and Karen and Therese started laughing so much we just couldn't stop. We just couldn't stop and Mrs Brown told us to "shut up" [*laughs*]. All through class and we were, oh it was just so funny. And I always feel so different from everyone else. 'Cause you know I don't have much clothes, I don't have many shoes like them. And you know they have really coloured ( ) and everything . . . And because they're all skinny and everything and I'm fat . . .

You see in the background of that one [*pointing to photo*]—oh, and there's another one, there. Well, I always get scared of those boys—I mean they're no big thing or anything, it's just that I feel so different you know, that they could say something about me.

Chas: What, you feel really vulnerable?

Jennifer: Mmmm.

Chas: In what way, physically or emotionally? How do you mean? Do you think they're going to physically hurt you or—

Jennifer: No, no—

Chas: emotionally hurt you—

Jennifer: I'd physically hurt them more than they could me.

Chas: . . . I wonder what it is then?

Jennifer: If they said something about me I'd feel, you know, quite bad.

Chas: . . . this thing of outward appearance is very important to you, isn't it?

Jennifer: Mmmm. I believe what other people say about me . . . [My friends] are a lot moodier than me and if I show my moody side then it all rocks. 'Cause I thrive on being cheerful and it's a lot nicer than being all sulky. And you know, mixed up with your own feelings. It feels a lot better as well, 'cause you know sitting like this on the bench in the playground and after a minute you get totally bored and wish you were with your friends smiling and being cheerful. . . . Therese who's, she's not really really skinny or anything and um, she's sort of got a half model build you know and sort of like that and she you know goes around calling me "fatty," although she is quite, really quite close really, but you know she doesn't realize that she's so skinny that it wouldn't hurt if someone called her fat and if anyone does call her fat and you know Stacey goes, "You're not exactly that skinny Therese," she goes, "Yes I am" . . . (Eastern Public—conversation with Jennifer)

Jennifer is *afraid* of what the boys might say *because she will believe them.* This is necessarily so since they will speak her into existence through the same discourses through which she speaks herself into existence. She has no alternative discursive practices with which to resist their speaking. Her central strategy is to avoid the storyline in which she can be positioned as marginal to the group. Her preferred storyline is of the pleasure of being with her friends, of laughing, smiling, and being cheerful. It is the achievement of this storyline that leads to the irrepressible energy of shared laughter that disrupts Mrs. Brown's classroom order. This is her major defense against the awfulness of being alone, of being not like her friends, not liked, of vulnerability in the face of words spoken about her. The self is revealed here, not as an object or thing, but as an interactive, discursive *process*, fragile, capable of great pleasure in oneness with the group, in being competent within its terms, but also vulnerable to the discourses through which it is spoken and speaks itself into existence.

Being simultaneously the same and different (a member who knows and takes pleasure in the ways of the social group and who is as well a specific identifiable being) are difficult to hold in balance. The press towards sameness can be traumatic if the child loses control of the flow of action surrounding the difference. Claire, the daughter of a close friend, commenced school at the beginning of 1992. She had attended a child-care center for several years and so was well used to, and competent in terms of, many of the features of schooling (Kantor, 1988). She nevertheless had a series of unexpected and traumatic events occur in the first week of school in relation to her positioning within the new group. In the summer holidays before school began, Claire had her hair cut in a short, stylish, "unisex" fashion. In the ensuing weeks she was somewhat taken aback when some people mistook her for a boy. At the same time, many people commented on how nice her hair looked. I told her about an article I had read in which the claim is made that in the world of art, the highest ideals of beauty have been closely linked with indeterminate sex. I suggested that she take claims that she looked like a boy as a claim that she was in this exceptional category. On arriving at school, however, she found herself seriously persecuted by a number of older girls who claimed that she was a boy and that she should go to the boys' toilet. In effect, the children were insisting that if she had a "boyish" hairstyle, she must also have male genitals. She should therefore have her right to enter the place where people with female genitals go without comment withdrawn from her. The obviousness of her category membership was questioned while the children worked to maintain the meaningfulness for themselves of the binary categories "male" and "female." The segregated toilets provide a material, architectural sign of male and female as exclusive categories. Moreover, they are, in this instance, categories that have strong implications for the actions of each individual. Social competence involves not simply knowing how to read the signs that signal which toilet is female and which is male, but also knowing the implications for action of these signs. One door can be entered, and the other is forbidden—behind it lies that which may not even be seen. Knowing whether one has got it right depends on the visibility of everyone else getting it right, yet genitals are hidden behind clothes. People whose gender is not immediately obvious create an uncertainty in the correct reading of signs. The assigning of meaning to the pictures or words on the door is necessarily a collective action. Otherwise, the signs have no meaning and the taboo cannot function. As a member of the collective, Claire too must be able to read the signs and practice in terms of the taboo. At the same time, she has access to another discourse about the acceptability of short hair for girls and for defining the categories male and female as other than absolutely exclusive and opposite. She nevertheless found it traumatic to be so loudly hailed by older girls as one who is incompetent, as one who does not know how to constitute herself as a legitimate person in the everyday world of her new school.

Confronted by these taunts and jeers, Claire might have succumbed to the category maintenance work being done, and positioned herself as unequivocally female, as opposite to male, as acceptable within the discourse of the taunters. She might, on the other hand, have attempted to pass as male. Or she could have positioned herself, as she did, as one who sees and rejects the narrow-mindedness of people who perceive gender in this way. What she cannot avoid, however, is the experience of having been hailed as transgressive, of not having unremarked or obvious membership.

The process of subjectification, then, entails a tension between simultaneously becoming a speaking, agentic subject and the corequisite for this, being subjected to the meanings inherent in the discourses through which one becomes a subject.

Identity: A story that can never fully be told

Most theories of "identity" dwell on the interaction between oneself and others, attributing much power to those others in their naming or shaping of the emergent self. Yet as Althusser (1984) points out, in modern(ist) conceptions of the person, one is *always already* a subject, even before birth. Prior to any interaction, the concept of the child as a being with individuality is already established. The child is hailed as such when it is born, and eventually comes to greet or hail itself in the same way, using the same discourses and storylines that it comes to take up as its own. Lacan (1966) has added an important shift to Althusser's idea of the humanist subject "always already" having been. He talks instead of the "inconclusive futurity of what will-always-already-have-been," or in other words, a recognition that the story of who we take ourselves to be can never be concluded. The story of who we are can never fully be told, since at any future point the apparent certainties of the present can be re-visited and re-viewed. Because of this reflexive feature of knowing, any experience of oneself exists in a " 'time' which can never be entirely remembered, since it will never fully have taken place" (Weber, 1991, p. 9). In this way Lacan moves away from the deterministic element of Althusser's subject and focuses more on the processes of always becoming.

To illustrate this point about the necessarily inconclusive nature of who we each are, I draw on an experience of my own in relation to my father. When he died recently, this was an unexpectedly traumatic event for me. Unexpected, because I did not think I was in any sense close to him. His children were, by his definition, the responsibility and interest of their mother. He required of her only that she alert him to their activities if they were going seriously astray, at which point he might intervene with a lecture and in some cases a controlling action. I wept at his death, a seemingly endless weeping, as much for the absence of love between us as for the fact that he was now dead. Some months later I came across a photograph I had never seen before of my father holding a small baby and looking at it with great tenderness. My mother had placed it in a bag of oddments she thought I might want. I could not imagine that this baby in the photograph was me. I had never experienced my father either holding me or looking at me tenderly. Perhaps the photo was actually of my younger brother, John, and my mother had made a mistake? But she insisted, when I asked her, that it was of me. My story of always having been unloved by my father, of being born into a family in which the father did not understand fatherhood to involve any form of tenderness, was called in question by this small, faded grey and white image.

For days, even weeks, I was obsessed by the photo, not knowing how to incorporate it into my idea of my life. Even if he had only held me and looked at me in that way once for the purposes of the photo, and at no other time, I could not maintain the certainty that he was who he had been for me until that point. I wanted to know, now, what had happened, how a man capable of looking like that became the man I knew. What he had always been, was no longer. My reading of the photo shifted who he was into an inconclusive futurity, even after his death.

What I now saw was someone else who had come to exist, not only in the present, but in a now always present past. As for myself, a possible new perception of a person emerged who did not need to be defined primarily through lack of love. Maybe I could begin to see myself as someone who had in fact always been loved, though troubled by a perceived lack of it from my father. Who I had always been now emerged too, in the present, as quite a different person. This was not because I discovered from the photo that I "really" had been loved by my father. It probably was just that once, for the eye of the camera, that I was held and looked at in that way. Rather, my interrogation of the image in the photograph opened up the possibility of a new

storyline that unhooked the old story of lack and put another, more abundant, enabling story in its place. I also realized, on reading of Barthes's struggle to find a "true" image/essence of his mother in photographs of her after her death, that my photograph was perhaps a means of ending the excess of my grief: grief at a lifetime of no love—no shared memories, no shared laughter, no shared intimacy. My father and I (unlike Barthes, whose memories seemed totally made up out of love) had given each other little more than the fact of a father, the fact of a second daughter. To find one moment of tenderness in the photograph, this I can choose to hold, not as a false representation of the whole, but as a moment that punctures the wholeness of the absence and alleviates the grief (Barthes, 1984).

To return to Althusser's image of hailing, then, the hailer does not *cause* the persons so hailed to see themselves in a particular way. My father did not cause me to feel loved by looking at me tenderly on the occasion of the photo, nor did he cause me to feel unloved by not doing so on other occasions. Both the person hailed and the person doing the hailing are constituted through discourses and storylines, the constitutive power lying in the discourse and the ways in which it has been taken up. Sometimes discourses are shared. Other times they are not. My father had a discourse about fatherhood that kept him separate from me. I made that separation central in my emotional life through psychological discourses that defined it as a crippling lack. I longed for something that I perceived myself not to have had. I was hailed through one discourse and recognized myself through another. There were, at the same time, many shared discourses about the meaning of being a person, about justice, about gender, and about class, through which my father and I managed to hail each other as knowable others, as father and daughter.

In order to know that one is being hailed as a subject, or as a particular kind of subject, in order to respond to that hailing, it is necessary to share some obviousnesses about the nature of persons and the processes in which they are engaged. Each person must make their way inside the experience of belonging to the category of person as that is understood within their time and culture if they are to recognize themselves when addressed as such. It is also, as Lacan (1966) has pointed out, a process in which one must have an *image* of oneself as subject, to know oneself as such. Like a photograph, one's image of one's bodily self has a sense of being fixed and bounded, and it can thus become a signifier of who one is. The fiction of a bounded unitary self, of a separate essential being, is established, through such images and through discourse, as real. At the same time as I learn to see other selves as they are spoken into existence, I learn to share in that speaking and in the speaking of "myself" into existence.

The achievement of oneself as a speaking subject can be extraordinarily painful and alienating. It can also be a highly pleasurable experience. Virginia Woolf (1976, p. 75) claims that her first and most important memory is an ecstatic awareness of herself experiencing sound and sight:

> [M]y other memory, which also seems to be my first memory, and in fact is the most important of all my memories . . . is of lying half asleep, half awake, in bed in the nursery at St Ives. It is of hearing the waves breaking, one, two, one, two, and sending a splash of water over the beach; and then breaking, one, two, one, two, behind a yellow blind. It is of hearing the blind draw its little acorn across the floor as the wind blew the blind out. It is of lying and hearing this splash and seeing this light, and feeling, it is almost impossible that I should be here; of feeling the purest ecstasy I can conceive.

For me, prior to the discovery of the photo, whenever I have tried to stretch my mind back as far as it will go, or when I have asked myself the question, if I were to write an autobiography, where would it begin, I think of the painful mental and physical harassment that was part of everyday life with my older brother Tony. But just as vivid is a particular memory of the flowering plum tree in my garden, which seems somehow to mark the beginning of my own awareness of myself as an experiencing subject. I think I was four or five. It was spring. It was a weekend and there was a sense of freedom and pleasure in the emergent day without plan or structure. I was in the sunlit garden and I think the grass was wet with the early morning dew. I noticed that the flowering plum tree was a profusion of blossoms and bees. I went up close to the blossoms and noticed their color and shape and smell for the first time. It was a miraculous discovery, in the garden by myself, amazed at the exquisite flowers and the thronging profusion of bees. It was the tinge of plum brown color in the flowers and the stalks that was most extraordinary given their pale delicate pink. I was, at the same time, intensely aware of myself standing there in the garden seeing and smelling the blossoms.

Layered behind that ecstatic image is another image of my father. He had lopped the tree back severely during the winter. Its shape was ugly and stunted. So there is in fact an earlier image of an ugly stuntedness by which I was affronted and to which I was opposed. The profusion of blossoms, I had been told by my mother, would come from the pruning. And here they were. My own for that moment.

And so we begin to create our own individual biographies, the stories through which there is an "I" with something to tell, but with stories that can never fully be told. Those unfolding, shifting stories are embodied through smell and touch, through sight and sound. They are lived with more than the conscious mind. What poststructuralist theorizing enables us to see is that the very specificity of those experiences, and their intensity, need not be the markers of a bounded self, but, rather, the moments at which an experiencing being comes to know the possibilities being made available by virtue of their presence within the collectivity, albeit a collectivity that constitutes itself through discourses in which the individual experiencing subject is made the primary focus.

Taking up discursive practices as one's own, and the possibility of agency

The children in *Shards of Glass* talked about themselves as becoming particular kinds of persons. They sometimes defined this as a series of choices made out of the possibilities they found in their immediate environment. These "choices" were in terms of assent or dissent, being like or not being like particular people. They were aware of the simultaneous power of others in their lives, and of moments they experienced as choice. These choices were made meaningful in terms of the discursive practices through which they had taken up their being and in terms of their positioning within categories made real through those discursive practices. Having taken on as one's own the discursive practices through which these memberships are articulated, the knowledge of how to belong in that category and the desire to be correctly located, no matter how painful that might be, are read as coming from one's "inner" self. Woolf (1976, p. 82) describes one such moment of "choice" in which she came to know her own powerlessness in contrast to her brother's power:

> Week after week passed at St Ives and nothing made any dint upon me. Then for no reason that I know about there was a sudden violent shock; something happened so violently that I have remembered it all my life. . . . I was fighting with Thoby on the lawn. We were pommelling each other with our fists. Just as I raised my fist to hit him, I felt: why hurt another person? I dropped my hand instantly, and stood there, and let him beat me. I remember the feeling. It was a feeling of hopeless sadness. It was as if I became aware of something terrible; and of my own powerlessness. I slunk off alone, feeling horribly depressed.

The question "why hurt another person?" is owned by the child, Virginia, as her own, as is the overwhelming experience of powerlessness that follows. The question belongs to "I." It is asked by "I," felt by "I." The I-as-girl is not articulated but nonetheless achieved. The desire for physical power and dominance is abandoned. Subjectification takes place in such a way that "identity" is shaped through "choices" that are understood to spring from and confirm that very identity, rather than through the apprehension of the discursive practices through which identity, personal choice, and inner and outer selves are made thinkable, achievable.

The following collective biography story, told by a young woman who was taking a course I was teaching on gender in New York State, provides an explicit example of desire being shaped in accordance with the gender categories to which one finds oneself assigned. It is also possible to see how apparently innocent *practices* that presuppose a gendered social structure can play a significant part in re-creating that gendered structure. It is in the particular moment captured by this story that her brother's penis, and therefore his membership in the category "male," comes to be associated with his competence, dominance, and power. The binary discourses through which her subjectification takes place make her brother's power specifically not her own, since, as girl, she is other-than-male, other-than-one-who-is-powerful. She achieves herself in this moment as girl. That is, she achieves herself as not powerful, and more significant, as *not desiring* power.

> I don't remember exactly how old I am, but I must have been pretty young because my brother, Max, and I still took baths together. Each night we would urinate before going into the tub. I had never expressed any interest before, but tonight I realized how fascinating it was that Max could urinate standing up. I watched with obvious delight as he controlled the direction and force of the

flow and pretended to bomb submarines in the toilet. He was clearly enjoying himself, and, as always, I wanted to play. I threw pieces of paper in the toilet and Max soaked them instantly. When it came to be my turn to urinate, I decided to try it standing up, like Max. I didn't know quite how to position myself. First I tried standing up just as Max had, but my little trickle missed the bowl completely. Then I tried squatting over the toilet. This time I managed to get it all in, but not with anywhere near the same amount of force and accuracy Max had exhibited. I most certainly couldn't aim at targets like he had, and I didn't have a penis to hold on to to control my stream. Whatever it was that I had, and I didn't know the name of it, was clearly inadequate. I was envious of the power and control Max had over his genitals. I was disappointed that we could only play the game when he was around, too. I cleaned up the floor and we got in the tub.

While we played in the tub that evening, my attention was predominantly focused on Max's penis. There it was in plain view. I felt different from him tonight, unlike I ever had. He assumed his usual position in the back of the tub so he could slide down on the incline and create waves for his toy boats. The object of his game was to shoot down any of my toys with his, or to go under the water for a sneak attack. Maybe it was just because he was bigger, older, and stronger, but he always managed to win. I felt dominated by him, almost powerless. The only way I could win was by outsmarting him, and then he would cheat. No matter how hard I tried, I'd never win. Why should I even bother to try? (Collective biography workshop)

Apparently harmless social rituals such as that of males urinating standing up and females urinating sitting down, combined with the binary divisions in the discourses through which male and female subjectivities are achieved, can thus be seen to constitute the experience of male superiority and female inferiority. The boy's penis is something that is named, recognized, touchable, and usable, not only for urinating but also for play, and in this case for powerful play, making clear the usually symbolic connection between penises and powerful destructive missiles. This particular practice provides Max with a powerful subject position that he can take up, with his penis as central to that power. He *recognizes* himself as powerful and uses that power in the ensuing play. In contrast, Jean's attempts at urinating standing up or squatting fail. She has no named, known, touchable part of herself that she can use in her efforts: "Whatever it was that I had, and I didn't know the name of it, was clearly inadequate." Jean's lack of aim seemed "natural," that is, to do with the physiology of her body. She did not realize boys' aim is the result of much practice, often with not very successful outcomes, and that girls can learn to hold their labia in such a way that their aim and force is at least equal to any boy's. Without access to this information and this practice, her powerlessness was understood in relation to an absence, a lack, a no-name.

> Silence itself—the things one declines to say, or is forbidden to name, . . . is less the absolute limit of discourse, the other side from which it is separated by a strict boundary, than an element that functions alongside the things said, with them and in relation to them within over-all strategies. (Foucault, 1980, p. 27)

Haug et al., writing about the collective biography or memory work they undertook in Germany, also discuss silence, and in particular the silences that surround female genitals. Following a story in which a girl talks about the struggle to learn to keep her legs together as "good girls" should, Haug et al. (1987, p. 77) say:

> Clearly, then, something "sexual" is being signified through leg posture. In expending such large amounts of energy on keeping our legs together, we begin to feel there is something we must keep hidden. . . . It is through the activity of concealment that meaning is generated. . . . "Sexualization" is acquired without sexuality itself ever being mentioned.

Thus the lack of naming, this sense of absence created around female genitalia, is also fundamental to the social practices through which femaleness is constituted. In fact, it is quite easy for women to urinate standing up, and, I am told, it is healthier for them to do so, because the bladder can empty itself more completely when the body is upright. Further, I have seen little girls beat their brothers in competitions to see who can pee the farthest out over the balcony. The labia can readily be shaped as a most effective spout by those whose female genitalia have not been constituted through absence, shame, and silence. I have found, however, that such information is generally greeted with disbelief, shock, or utter amazement. (I have even heard of distressed dog owners ringing in to a talk-back veterinary radio program about their "abnormal" male dog who does not cock his leg to urinate. The vet, taking their concern seriously, advised them to take the dog to a park where other male dogs were cocking their legs so that it could get the idea from watching them.)

Despite the fact that Jean desires the same skill as Max, she does not persevere with her attempts to get it right, assuming that her failure is proof of the powerlessness that is associated with her femaleness—her lack of a penis. She does not know how many failed attempts Max inevitably had before he got his act under control (nor probably does Max). As a result, not only does Jean observably, in this story, begin to withdraw from her desire to have the competence she sees Max displaying ("why should I even try"), but she associates the desire for power and dominance quite clearly with the male body, with something that is understood as "natural" rather than socially constituted. The "natural" power the male has is, by implication, unnatural for the girl. That which we take to be natural is very hard to understand as social, and even harder to understand as a ritual whose significance lies in the maintenance of the gender order. Through the telling of this story Jean has delved into her own subjectivity, and the group has come to see how genitals and gender are implicated in the social practices through which they have been constituted as male or female, as masculine or feminine, as powerful or powerless. They have also seen one of the ways that desire is shaped through and in relation to those practices. There is no need here for a psychoanalytic explanation. Jean understood male as powerful and female as powerless through the practical rituals and the semiotics of these, and the discursive practices (including the silences) through which those rituals were given meaning.

~

It is to the absences and silences in our talk, as well as to the discourses and practices through which they articulate their experience, that any analysis must look. In the chapters that follow in this book I explore and extend the concepts raised in this first chapter. These include in particular the concepts of desire, agency, positioning, subject and subjectivity, and power and powerlessness. These conceptual and theoretical explorations draw on, for their elaboration, my own embodied lived history of being in the world, and they draw on a number of studies in which the participants examine and discuss their discursive constitution of selves. It also draws on studies in which participants attempt to deconstruct, disrupt, and go beyond familiar, obvious, taken-for-granted practices. I begin with desire, and in particular my own desires as a feminist and as a woman.

3 ~ The problem of desire

A S A FEMINIST, I desire a world in which anyone's sex/gender[1] is made relevant only in the process of biological reproduction. I desire a world in which there are multiple ways of being available to everyone, that multiplicity not being organized around the male/female dualism. I long for a world in which each of us can move legitimately and recognizably from any one of those multiple ways of being to another. I long for the "female" ways of being that are available to me now to be valued and available to anyone.

As a woman, however, my desires often run counter to this. My desires are organized in terms of storylines and metaphors in which my femaleness is a central feature. If I were the kind of unitary rational being that liberal humanists once convinced most of us we were, then to the extent that my "feminist" desire contradicts "feminine" desire, the feminist would undo the feminine. But our patterns of desire are organized around and in terms of our gendered identity such that rational attention to the contradiction is not sufficient to undo it. Our being encompasses more than the post-Enlightenment rationality celebrated as fundamental to "man." We live with multiple contradictions, and the contradiction between femininity and feminism is one of these (Moi, 1989).

Desire goes beyond rationality and to a large extent is part of the mysterious, the poetic, the ineffable—in a realm not readily pinned down with words, not readily amenable to logic and rationality (Pearce, 1989). In various humanist guises, desire has been used as an indicator of who we "really" are, as signifying an essence that is "natural" and personal, as independent of social influence. But I argue here that desire is spoken into existence, it is shaped through discursive and interactive practices, through the symbolic and the semiotic. Desires are constituted through the narratives and storylines, the metaphors, the very language and patterns of existence through which we are "interpellated" into the social world (see Althusser, 1971). Desire, along with rational argument, evidence, storylines, and fantasy, are all implicated in our interpretation of ourselves and of others, and there are often contradictions between them. While we may find it hard to speak about desire—to pin it down—we may, through a feminist deconstruction of the storylines, metaphors, images, and practices through which we know who we are, come to quite different lived patterns of desire, patterns that no

---

This chapter was originally published in the journal *Social Problems* 37(4) in 1990.

longer lock us in to the "feminine" or the "masculine" but allow a movement amongst a multiplicity of ways of being (Davies, 1989a).

It is to an understanding of how desires are constituted as central in each person's gendered identity that this chapter is directed. This chapter, however, is not just about desire. It is a search for, a playing with, a new way of speaking and writing that opens the possibility of encompassing, even embracing, opposite and contradictory positions in understanding selves in relation to the social world. To introduce this idea I use Kristeva's (1986 [1981]) paper, "Women's Time," in which she discusses the three "generations" of feminism and argues that the current generation of feminists must take up all of these feminisms, despite the contradictions between them. I then go on to argue that the means for moving beyond the old ways of thinking and speaking do not lie with psychoanalysis (Kristeva's view), but first with an analysis both of how existing discursive practices trap us into the worlds we are trying to move beyond, and second with the collective development of discursive practices that bring into being those new, almost unimaginable possibilities that are being opened up by some feminist theorists and also feminist fiction writers. Fundamental to this idea is an understanding of the person as process, and of words coming not from an essential core but from the discursive practices through which the person is constituting themselves and being constituted.

Kristeva's "three generations" of feminism: Beyond the male/female dualism

One of the old ways of speaking that this paper attempts to move beyond is the reduction of the person through the process of categorization. Classifying oneself and others, and being classified, are interesting and dangerous processes, because classification can be a way of controlling, of reducing, of slotting someone into that which is already known. It is a way of linking the identity of the speaker or writer with the words spoken or written. A central concern of feminism is precisely to avoid such reduction. Yet classification, or labeling, also provides a way of understanding diversity and complexity and is, as well, fundamental to any political action.

Kristeva's (1986 [1981]) three "generations" of feminism and her elaboration of the relation between them shows how we might move beyond the liberal humanist version of "Enlightenment man" and his associated laws of rationality that insist on unitary selves or linear thought and on apparently natural classifications. She does not mean these as generations in a linear time sense but rather as *signifying spaces,* each being "both a corporeal and desiring mental space" (p. 209). She avoids the dangers of essentializing by allowing, even encouraging, feminists to occupy the signifying space of all three of the feminisms despite their profound contradictions: "so it can be argued that as of now a third attitude is possible, thus a third generation which does not exclude—quite the contrary—the *parallel* existence of all three in the same historical time, or even that they be interwoven one with the other" (Kristeva, 1986 [1981]). These three generations, which appeared at historically distinct periods and which now exist in parallel, interwoven as corporeal desiring spaces, are:

1. Liberal feminism—desire for access to the male symbolic order;

2. Radical feminism—celebration of femaleness and of difference, desire for separation from the male symbolic order;

3. The desire for an imagined possibility of "woman as whole," not constituted in terms of the male/female dualism. Such a move involves confronting one's own personal identity with its organization of desire around "masculinity" or "femininity." The desired end point of such a confrontation is to de-massify maleness and femaleness—to reveal their multiple and fragmented nature and remove from the meaning of maleness and femaleness any sense of opposition, hierarchy, or necessary difference. This is not a move towards sameness but towards multiple ways of being. It is the feminist desire with which I began this paper.[2]

Kristeva suggests that socialist feminists, while also seeking to go beyond difference, found that they were received by men only on male terms, either as feminine/sexual other, or as male. It is the tenacious presence of this familiar dynamic that drives the deconstructive/reconstitutive work of feminists in the third desiring space.

Kristeva's is a radical position to take up, since these feminisms are in many ways profoundly contradictory and it is hard to believe in them or think them in the same space. She holds that although they appeared at different historical moments, they each still are relevant in different contexts since they serve different purposes and can achieve quite different things. The essentialism of much radical feminism, for example, in which femininity is celebrated, is totally at odds with the third generation in which femininity is seen as a metaphysical construction to be wrestled with and moved beyond. It is equally radical to adopt the poststructuralist/postmodernist stance in which the source of one's words are not one's self, nor are those words indicators of who one "really" is. In the third desiring space one recognizes that the words one utters, and the interactive practices in which one engages, do not gain their meanings through any individual's intentions. Rather it is through the discursive and interactive practices that we are interpellated into the collective and through which we become speaking subjects.

We take the words we speak to be our own at the same time that they speak us into existence.

Adopting this attitude, if we find ourselves in a situation in which access of women to an area previously denied them is the issue, engaging in that fight for access does not signify that we *are* liberal feminists in some essentialist sense, but simply that we are speaking subjects who can mobilize concepts of justice and equality whenever anyone is denied access based on the genitals they happen to have. Similarly, in a situation in which what it means to be female is downgraded, radical feminist strategies and concepts may be used to counteract that downgrading, or, if a group of women friends sit around talking and laughing about the superiority of the way women do things and the absolute hopelessness of the "male" way, this does not necessarily mean they are asserting an essentialist view of maleness and femaleness and the necessity of the division of the world into (superior) females and (inferior) males. Rather they may be asserting the right to claim their way of doing things as of value in a world where these are constantly being downgraded. In a world that was not divided into males and females, or in a world where femaleness was not downgraded, the celebration of femaleness would not be necessary. Those qualities would be some amongst many that were valued and applauded. But we do not live in such a world and so radical feminist discourse is necessary. To be operating in the third desiring space is to recognize just this multiple nature of the self and its capacity to enter into a range of contradictory discourses.

A major contribution to feminist debate in the third space is the recognition that sexism is not just "out there"—it is not simply "society's" rules and regulations that lie at the heart of the problem, or sexist people who deny us our rights (though certainly these are part of the problem). Sexism is also taken up by each of us in the process of taking ourselves up as gendered beings. As Butler (1997, p. 14) says:

> Power acts on the subject in at least two ways: first, as what makes the subject possible, the condition of its possibility and its formative occasion, and second, as what is taken up and reiterated in the subject's own acting.

We perceive the world from a gendered subject position and we re-create the sexist world by re-creating the male/female dualism in the things we say and do. The idea that male and female difference is the unproblematic base on which gender is built is seriously questioned in this third space. Sex, too, is recognized as in large part a discursive production. At the same time, in coming to see how gendered subjectivity is developed, the possibility of change, or to use Kristeva's term, de-massification, is opened up. The bonds of compulsory heterosexuality are one element of the male/female dualism that can be readily questioned both within a radical feminist discourse (in which femaleness is celebrated independently of maleness) as well as in the third space (in which the sex/gender of oneself and the other are no longer taken to be central defining features of persons).

For Kristeva, desire is central to who any one person is, not in the sense of what we "really want" indicating who we "really are," but in the sense that in being discursively constituted in certain ways, it is the patterns of desire that we learn in that construction that will hold us there, despite any rational wish that this not be the case. We must look, she says, to the re-constitution of ourselves outside the mass of *woman*ness or *man*ness. We must look to the organization of desire, not in terms of our assigned sex/gender but in terms of the multiple possibilities that being a person opens up.

Language and desire

Kristeva's understanding of desire is embedded in her interest in psycho-analysis, which she uses as a discourse to make sense of, to find a path through and beyond, maleness and femaleness. While I share her vision of the de-massification of difference, I find psychoanalysis one more individu-alistic discourse in which femininity is defined in terms of a lack that must be struggled with. Instead I want to stress the importance of collectively posi-tioning ourselves in relation to language. That is, through recognizing the constitutive force of discourse, rather than seeing it merely as a tool for describing a real world, we can see ourselves as being spoken into existence. We also can see both the potency of speaking in new ways and the possibil-ity of refusing old, undesirable ones. This is not an individual but rather a collective task, though the possibilities it opens up may be experienced as a profound personal liberation.

The shift away from the unitary self, the "I" whose words come from and signal an essential self, towards an "I" who can be recognized as both multi-ple and collectively, discursively produced was for me a profoundly liberat-ing shift. It gave me for the first time a clear voice, a sense of myself as a speaking subject with authority, rather than one who was in error for pre-suming to speak or who was constantly required to cover up those gaps and contradictions that had always been the focus of my gaze. I could now speak from my embodied knowledges, contradictory as they were, and could see how I could mobilize existing discourses to say what I wanted to say. My desire to speak, and the competence to do so, was in large part an interpel-lation of myself into the third space through poststructuralist discourse.

Poststructuralist discourse makes it possible to imagine finding new ways of speaking that allow us to articulate the multiplicity of our experiencing selves, our subjectivities. It is possible to imagine locating ourselves not as halves of a metaphysical dualism, not as divided off from each other according to the genitals we happen to have, each half taking its meaning in opposition to the other, each needing/desiring the other to fill its own lack, but rather as beings capable of developing new storylines, new metaphors, new images through which we can live our lives. This is necessarily a collective process in which new discourses are both generated and heard as meaningful, as livable, and through which unwanted patterns of desire can be displaced. Cixous (1981, 1986), Haug et al. (1987), Irigaray (1985), and Kristeva (1986 [1981]) are central figures in this process, and the work of Grosz (1989), Moi (1987), and Weedon (1987), among many others, provides clear access to these discourses.

Cixous (1981, p. 262), in articulating her desire to experience a kind of loving made possible in a world without the male/female division, deconstructs and moves beyond the psychoanalytic model, both in its heterosexual assumptions and in its notion of desire based on lack:

> I want all. I want all of me with all of him. Why should I deprive myself of part of us? I want all of us. Woman of course has a desire for a "loving desire", and not a jealous one. But not because she is gelded; not because she is deprived and needs to be filled out, like some wounded person who wants to console herself or seek vengeance. I don't want a penis to decorate my body with. But I do desire the other for the other, whole and entire, male or female; because living means wanting everything that is, everything that lives, and wanting it alive. Castration? Let others toy with it. What's a desire originating from a lack? A pretty meager desire.

These words, for me, capture a central possibility of Kristeva's (1986 [1981], p. 209) new generation of feminists who

> having started with the idea of difference, . . . will be able to break free of [their] belief in Woman, Her power, Her writing, so as to channel this demand for difference into each and every element of the female whole, and finally to bring out the singularity of every woman, and beyond this her multiplicities, her plural languages, beyond the horizon, beyond sight, beyond faith itself?

A fundamental struggle within feminist consciousness is between ways of speaking that constitute women as *essentially* women, and those that reject this notion of essence and the male/female dualism. Though the quote from Kristeva seems to give weight to the latter, the very words she (inevitably) uses speak back into existence the former. What it means to be "whole" yet still "woman" when woman means other to man and whole means constituting one's self independently of any man, or of the concept man, is a fundamental contradiction struggled with by each feminist, each feminism.

Cixous rejects that element of psychoanalysis that sees femaleness inevitably constituted as a lack in relation to maleness.

Psychoanalysis has opened up, has given us a way of attending to, that aspect of human experience that is not rational. Like fiction, psychoanalysis calls in question the boundaries between the "real" and the "not real"; it challenges the viability of rationally constituted binary oppositions, and it foregrounds the personal, which is usually backgrounded in academic discourses. The problem with psychoanalysis, for me, is that it generates a story of oneself that essentializes femininity as formed in relation to the phallogocentric father. This is only a valuable story if it can be displaced with another—a story of femaleness as a wholeness that is not constituted within the male/female dualism, such a story finding ways of inscribing itself in the constitutive practices of the collectives of which we are members.

In the new relationship with language that I want to elaborate here as an alternative route to psychoanalytic discourse, our speaking/writing can be understood as each of us mobilizing a variety of discourses within different contexts and for different purposes. We can take up and put down the different subject positions available within these discourses, our subjectivity always fluid and in process. Our energy will not be taken up with blocking out that which does not fit some imaginary ideal of the unitary rational non-contradictory self, but rather we can expand in the excitement of discovering *all* that we might be and of speaking that into existence.

Thus the speaking/writing that I do in my attempts to move towards the imagined possibility of multiplicity is essentially Foucauldian:

> Discourses, in Foucault's work, are ways of constituting knowledge, together with the social practices, forms of subjectivity and power relations which inhere in such knowledges and the relations between them. Discourses are more than ways of thinking and producing meaning. They constitute the "nature" of the body, unconscious and conscious mind and emotional life of the subjects they seek to govern. Neither the body nor thoughts and feelings have meaning outside their discursive articulation, but the ways in which discourse constitutes the minds and bodies of individuals is always part of a wider network of power relations, often with institutional bases. (Weedon, 1987, p. 108)

If in contrast we see language as merely a tool for describing, then sex/gender can only be seen as a natural fact of human existence. Poststructuralist theorizing liberates us from this "natural attitude" to language and opens up a space in which we can play with and speak/write ourselves into an imaginary world in which we are all. At the same time, poststructuralist discourse enables us to see how imagination is caught and contained, and old thinking re-established, since the constitutive force of other and current ways of speaking speak back into existence that which we seek to move beyond. Cixous (1986, p. 83) writes that

> men and women are caught up in a web of age-old cultural determinations that are almost unanalyzable in their complexity. One can no more speak of "woman" than of "man" without being trapped within an ideological theatre where the proliferation of representations, images, reflections, myths, identifications transform, deform, constantly change everyone's Imaginary and invalidate in advance any conceptualization.

To break that hold we need to examine that which is "almost unanalyzable" and through recognizing it as discursively/interactively/collectively constituted and therefore as amenable to change, we can begin to move towards an imaginary ideal through speaking/writing it into existence.

Becoming a person

What it means to be an individual person in the "modern" world involves taking on *as our own* the very discursive practices through which we are constituted. Rather than seeing those discursive practices as external and coercive, we take ourselves up as speaking subjects, claiming authorship of the texts we speak. In doing so we fail to recognize the constitutive and coercive force of the very words we speak. It is the (mis)taking of ourselves as authors that Althusser (1971) refers to as the process of interpellation. This involves far more than learning ways of speaking about what appears to be a real world. We learn categories of people and who is excluded and included in these, e.g., male/female, father/daughter. We learn how to participate in the discursive practices that give meaning to those categories, including the storylines in which various subject positions are elaborated. We learn, more important, how to position ourselves in terms of those categories and storylines as though we, in fact, are in one category rather than another (e.g., as girl and not boy, or as "good" girl and not "bad" girl). Finally we come to see ourselves as having those characteristics that locate us in these different categories, as belonging in the world in certain ways and thus seeing it accordingly. Through this latter process, we become emotionally committed to our category memberships and experience our belonging and not belonging in moral terms.

In this process of self-acquisition, pronoun grammar gives a person an illusion of being a historically continuous, unitary entity separate from the social world. As such, our emotions and desires are experienced as emanating from a more fundamental, essential level of self and as indicators of who we really are. We take ourselves as responsible for the words we "choose" and for their effects in the apparently preexisting, material world. We achieve this way of seeing and being so successfully that it is extraordinarily difficult to retrieve a perception of ourselves as continually being constituted by and through our "own" discursive practices. It is in the context of this process that the experience of contradiction becomes a fruitful site for feminist poststructuralist theory to examine and understand what it means to be a gendered person.

Just as in the stories told in books, there are certain unquestioned features of *lived* narratives. These include, for example, that each character will be identifiably male or female and will not only always have been that particular sex, but will remain so. Fictional stories in which there are changes from one to the other, as in Woolf's (1971) *Orlando* or Le Guin's (1983) *Left Hand of Darkness,* are generally not considered to be about "real" people. Real people who wish this change require surgical intervention, so central are genitals taken to be to sex/gender. There are some things that one might imagine in a story but that are difficult if not impossible to achieve as a real-life story as they are currently understood. Your sex at birth is what you must remain. This creation of an absolute out of something that is far from an absolute difference biologically (Connell, 1987; Davies, 1989a; Kessler and McKenna, 1978) is in large part an achievement of lived and told narratives. That is, being identifiably male or female is not only observably the way people are in the everyday world, but it is also the way people could imaginably be in any world we could think of, at least prior to the development of feminist poststructuralist writing.

Our lived narratives are in part a result of our original assignment to one sex or the other, but they are also the means whereby that original assignment is confirmed, made real, achieved as an accomplishment in the everyday world. In my research with preschool children (Davies, 1989a), those who made this feature of their genderedness most visible were those ill at ease with the storylines available to their sex.

Joanne, a four-year-old, was not at all happy with the storylines available to girls. She enjoyed the kinds of games that the "macho" group of boys engaged in—fairly dominant, powerful, controlling kinds of games—and she wanted access to those games, not as the female, the *other* to their male, but as one of them, the heroes of their play. At the same time she was extremely socially competent and never in any doubt that she was obliged to achieve herself as identifiably female. She moved competently and strongly, like a boy, but to prevent people mistaking her for a boy she tied her hair up in a girlish topknot. The boys would not often give her access to their games in the way she wanted. Once, when they were playing Voltron, a popular television show at that time, they had let her be the leader and she had had a wonderful time, but mostly they insisted she be the princess (the one who keeps falling off Voltron, becoming victim to the baddies and needing to be saved), and so she refused to join their play.

One occasion when Joanne had access to a powerful position in her play involved the appearance of a new tree house in the school yard. On that day, there was a hive of excited activity around the new tree house. There were only a small number of children who could competently climb the ladder up into the green leafy space. Then there were the rest who milled around at the bottom of the ladder, wanting to climb up, but not feeling competent or safe enough to do so. There was a feeling of tension and excitement amongst those who did climb. A small group of the macho boys declared the space to be a boys' space and that they had taken possession of it. The teachers, perhaps because I was watching, insisted that girls too were allowed in this space, even climbing into the space to assert the truth of their claim. Shortly afterwards, Joanne and her friend took possession. They had found a technique for preventing others from climbing up the ladder in a way that was invisible to the teachers. They dropped the sawdust, which had been left by the carpenters on the floor of the tree house, into the tentative, upward-looking faces of the people who were attempting to climb up the ladder, causing a rapid and noisy retreat that mystified the teachers. Joanne and Tony were deeply immersed in the power and excitement of their takeover of this highly desirable public space. Tony noticed me watching and chose to ignore me. Then Joanne saw me watching, and she paused and said, "I'm just cleaning the floor, there's all this sawdust the carpenters left here."

Whether this was simply "a story," or whether Joanne believed her description of what she was doing, is not really important. What is important is that she knew the correct, domestic narrative into which her activity *should* fit. Tony, in contrast, and like the group of macho boys before him, displayed an intense and undivided attention to the task of taking over the new territory. There was no hesitation, no visible question about the defensibility of his strategy for establishing his territory, and no need to explain to me, therefore, that he was "really" innocent. There was no sense of guilt to be explained away. Joanne was still able to proceed with the activity following her "explanation," but there was some hesitation, some experience of doubt about the legitimacy of her forceful, dominant action. She could not be, as Tony appeared to be, fully immersed in asserting herself in this way, at least while I was watching. To that extent she was being interpellated into the social world as correctly gendered.

Althusser (1971, pp. 162–63) used the concept of interpellation to describe a process whereby individuals *mistakenly* take themselves to be author of the ideological discourse through which various state apparatuses take them over:

> I shall then suggest that ideology "acts" or "functions" in such a way that it "recruits" subjects among the individuals (it recruits them all), or transforms the individuals into subjects (it transforms them all) by that very precise oper-

ation which I have called *interpellation* or hailing, and which can be imagined along the lines of the most commonplace everyday police (or other) hailing: "Hey, you there!"

It is the mistaken nature of individuals' beliefs that they are authors of their own meanings, and the imaginary (in Althusser's terms, false) nature of the identification with the value positions within those discourses that leads many poststructuralists to see the subject/author as dead. But the speaking *female* subject is far from dead. The idea that the subject is dead is only meaningful within a masculinist humanist understanding of the subject in which the individual and the collective are understood as separate and in an agonistic relationship. The individual male hero who rose above, conquered, was separate from, and who often fundamentally controlled and changed the collective might well be dead. The female subject, who is *of* the collective, who knows in connection to, rather than in separation from, is more alive than ever. Through poststructuralism she has her subjectivity confirmed—she claims her once-derided ways of knowing the world, her fragmented, contradictory, always unfolding, embodied knowing. Her subjectivity becomes, through shared discourses, her connection to the universal, rather than the dismissible opposite of "true," objective knowledge (Haug et al., 1987).

Within poststructuralist discourse, objective knowledge is understood as a fantasy of the Enlightenment, a fantasy through which woman knew her object status and her alienation from the possibility of knowing as one was supposed to know. And it is understood as a fantasy that men have used to heighten their own speaking status, and with which they have separated themselves off from themselves (Seidler, 1989). Women can use poststructuralist theory to name those "misrecognitions" of themselves that are constituted through phallogocentric discourse, and they can use that knowledge to construct discourses through which they can be recognized as they choose to be, those choices being knowingly informed by the value positions of a feminism that gives women the voice with which to speak their protest and to formulate their rebellion.

Thus the woman as subject may well be *subjected, fragmented, in process,* her body *inscribed* with cultural notions of what she should be. Her choices may well be "correct" in the terms of the available discourses. Her desires may well be the result of bodily inscription through metaphors and storylines that catch her up in one way of being/of desiring from which she has no escape. But now she can reinscribe, discover new storylines, invert, invent, break the bounds of old structures and old discourses. And this is precisely what feminist poststructuralist writers are doing. For them, poststructuralism need not offer the death of the subject/author, but rather the first recognition of the means by which they have been subjected, made object, deprived of agency, and inscribed with patterns of desire that hold all of this in place. Poststructuralist discourse offers a critique of the celebration and equation of masculinity and rationality and confirms for woman her sense of self as one who is embodied, whose emotions, desires, feelings are as legitimate a part of "reason" as the much-vaunted rationality she has supposedly lacked. Woman can be a subject who realizes, speaks, writes her subjected condition, and searches out the ways in which the patterns holding that subjection in place can be subverted, turned to her own ends. She can begin to reclaim herself as whole, entire, capable of loving not from lack or need, but from a desire located in the whole of her embodied being. She moves thus to a celebration of desiring—as opposed to being the desirable object—playing with new words, new patterns, new meanings, breaking up old patterns, old storylines, finding the texts of words, of body, of interaction that make the idea and the ideal of whole, embodied woman as active subject a lived reality.

Cixous claims that such multiple wholeness, although an ideal for everyone, is more likely to be achieved by women at this point in time than by men. Women have, through the work of the first generation of feminists, had access to male ways of being. Ironically, the insistence that they maintain their femininity while entering male domains, painful as this has been (de Beavoir, 1972; Riviere, 1986; Walkerdine, 1989), has nonetheless given them the knowledge that these hierarchical dualisms can be encompassed in one being, whereas men, in equating masculine with the rational, the nonemotional, and the nonfemale, have been denied that knowledge (Seidler, 1989). What poststructuralism opens up is the possibility of encompassing these contradictory ways of being with ease, even with pleasure. Such a position perfectly intertwines the second and third spaces of feminism, since it includes a recognition and celebration of female ways of knowing *and* a use of that knowing to work beyond femaleness and its relation to maleness.

The male/female dualism

Male and female are not just two different ways of being that at best are complementary and at worst engaged in a fight to the death. In taking oneself up as either male or female, within current discourses one is doing so *in relation to* the other. Cixous (1986, p. 63) elaborates the male/female division in terms of a set of binary oppositions: activity/passivity; sun/moon; culture/nature; day/night; father/mother; head/emotions; intelligible/sensitive; logos/pathos. Moi (1987, p. 104) describes how these dualisms are imbricated in the patriarchal value system:

> [E]ach opposition can be analysed as a hierarchy where the "feminine" side is always seen as the negative, powerless instance. . . . Western philosophy and

literary thought are and always have been caught up in this endless series of hierarchical binary oppositions that always in the end come back to the fundamental "couple" of the male/female.

The almost incomprehensible task in the third desiring space is to begin to break up these dualisms, and to disconnect them from the idea of persons who happen to have one or another set of genitals.

In the second space this involves the (re)construction of the "lesser" side as of value. Often this is done in a way that derides the male side of the binary divide and celebrates the female side. One of the most vivid dangers at this tier is that it plays precisely into the hands of the patriarchs by emphasizing and essentializing the difference. A patriarch disguised as a feminist, or at least as sympathetic to the feminist cause, can welcome this celebration of femaleness precisely because it keeps women as he wants them—other, and giving meaning to his masculinity.

A further and quite different (de)construction happens in the third space. Masculinity and femininity are removed from the equation, and both sides of what was once understood as part of a binary divide become something any person can and should have access to. But there is a complex set of conceptual shifts required before this becomes a meaningful possibility. These require not that men should be free to behave like women and vice versa but rather require an uncoupling of the concepts of masculinity/femininity and identity. These deconstructions in the second and third spaces, dangerous as one is and impossible as the other seems, and contradictory as they appear to be, are essential to the world that I imagine.

Androgyny and bisexuality were for some time happily embraced as the solution to the male/female divide. But two opposites that take their meaning in terms of each other are not easily summed. In her book *Let's Take Back Our Space,* Marianne Wex (1979) shows, through photographs, a consistent pattern of men sitting with legs apart and women sitting with legs together. The legs apart in a man look assertive, "manly." The legs together in a woman look beautiful, "womanly." Wex shows that the way that women sit, if adopted by a man, signals submissiveness. And that the way that men sit, if adopted by a woman, far from signaling assertiveness, signals sexual availability. Thus the members of one sex cannot simply appropriate the iconography of the other sex because the image is translated in terms of the sex of the user to mean something entirely different. For a woman to "behave like a man" does not mean the same thing as a man behaving like a man. Just examine the emotions and images that these two phrases call up as you contemplate them. "She is womanly" and "he is womanly." The characteristics being referred to by the word "womanly" are not the same in each phrase. "She" and "he" signal that an entirely different way of hearing is appropriate in each case. Cixous (1981, p. 254) argues that we need to think of an *other* form of bisexuality to get beyond this impasse.

> In saying "bisexual, hence neuter," I am referring to the classic conception of bisexuality, which squashed under the emblem of castration fear and along with the fantasy of a "total" being (though composed of two halves), would do away with the difference experienced as an operation incurring loss, as the mark of a dreaded sectility. To this self-effacing, merger-type bisexuality, which would conjure away castration . . . [,] I oppose the *other bisexuality* on which every subject not enclosed in the false theatre of phallogocentric representationalism has founded his/her erotic universe. Bisexuality: that is, each one's location in self (*reperage en soi*) of the presence—variously manifest and insistent according to each person, male or female—of both sexes, non-exclusion either of the difference or of one sex, and, from this "self-permission", multiplication of the effects of the inscription of desire, over all parts of my body and the other body.

Many feminists and nonfeminists alike balk at this third desiring space. They argue it is unnecessary, that we can simply move from bipolarity of sexes to bimodality. In this construction males and females are still two identifiable and separate groups who have some areas of overlap, some characteristics in common, and the virtues of each are celebrated. This is more comfortable, less threatening, and doesn't defy imagination in the way that the third space does. The third space is engaged in a shift through which the present, our history, and our literature will never appear the same again. I believe that bimodality will not work; it does not go far enough and will always allow a sliding back into the hierarchical dualisms in which it is rooted.

The "other bisexuality" that Cixous imagines does not reject difference, nor what we currently call masculinity or femininity. She does reject the limitations inherent in being *one or the other,* argues for multiplicity in difference, and seeks to move beyond the inevitable heterosexuality that holds the male/female dualism intact. The "bimodal" argument appears to be an easy solution—a freeing of the boundaries without having to do the serious work of (re)constructing one's identity, one's pattern of desire, around something other than one's sex/gender. But the bimodal model ignores two things. First, it ignores the politics of difference—the inscription of woman as other—not as one who desires but who is desired—the outrage of the feminine position. Second, it ignores the oppositional and relational nature of the concepts, and the impossibility of any simple transposition of emotion, of desire, of signifying practices from one to the other.

Wilshire (1989, pp. 95–96), in a study of myth, extends the list of the hierarchical dualisms associated with maleness and femaleness as follows:

KNOWLEDGE (accepted wisdom) / IGNORANCE (the occult and taboo)
higher up / lower down
good, positive / negative, bad
mind (ideas), head, spirit / body (flesh), womb (blood), nature (Earth)
reason (the rational) / emotions and feelings (the irrational)
cool / hot
order / chaos
control / letting things be, allowing, spontaneity
objective (outside, "out there") / subjective (inside, immanent)
literal truth, fact / poetic truth, metaphor, art
goals / process
light / darkness
written text, Logos / oral tradition, enactment, Myth
Apollo as sky-sun / Sophia as earth-cave-moon
public sphere / private sphere
seeing, detached / listening, attached
secular / holy and sacred
linear / cyclical
permanence, ideal (fixed) forms / change, fluctuations, evolution
"changeless and immortal" / process, ephemeras (performance)
hard / soft
independent, individual, isolated / dependent, social, interconnected, shared
dualistic / whole
MALE / FEMALE

She says that to move beyond these dualisms we must move away from binary logic. She quotes physicists who have recognized that far from the opposite of a truth always being a falsehood (a dualism), the opposite of a profound truth is often another profound truth (not a dualism). Thus, she says, "if the first-placed word in each dualism is profoundly true (e.g., literalness, mind, reason, cool, etc.) their opposites are also profoundly true (metaphor, body, emotion, hot, etc.)" (Wilshire, 1989, p. 105). It is, then, outside of logical argument, as this has been generally understood, that women can move towards wholeness. If we have been constituted on one half of this divide, that half taking its meaning in opposition to the other half, then the two cannot be added. It is only by learning to see them as nondualistic, not either/ors with one in the ascendant, but couplings, that we can begin to conceive the wholeness we might have if we were not constituted in terms of the dualisms: "Rather than choosing or demeaning one column or the other, I suggest we mine the *warmth* of women's experience and ways of knowing (*dark, interior, female* wisdom) as well as the *cool, bright, enlight*enment of public, male Apollo-Logos" (Wilshire, 1989, p. 96).

The organization of desire in relation to sex/gender

In the previous chapter I discussed the ways in which children learn the correct pattern of desire for their own gender, and how other children work on them to help them get it right. I illustrated this in particular with the story of Virginia Woolf finding herself no longer able or willing to hit her brother Thoby, and with the girl in the bathtub desiring power and then abandoning the desire as she came to see that power as resting somehow naturally in her brother's body. While the subjection of oneself through the discourses of gender, as in these stories, may be a "private" process, when done "incorrectly" it becomes a visible, collective, and public process whereby individuals are hailed as incorrect, as Claire was when she was told which toilets to go to, being told that they have misrecognized the positions that are available to them. Through such hailing individuals learn to correctly locate themselves in terms of the appropriate gendered subject positions or to accept as their own a marginal subject position. In the following conversation with a four-year-old boy, for example, we discuss a story in which a boy, Oliver Button, wanted to do "girls' things" and was teased by the other boys:

B.D.: So why doesn't Oliver Button like to play "boys' games"?
Robbie: Because he likes girls' things.
B.D.: Because he likes girls' things. Mmm. [*Reads about Oliver Button going to dancing school.*] So all the others are little girls, aren't they? [*Looking at picture.*]
Robbie: That's wrong.
B.D.: It's wrong, is it? So you wouldn't want Oliver to go? If you were Oliver and you hated all the boys' things and you wanted to do girls' things, would you want to go to dancing school?
Robbie: No.
B.D.: [*Reads about boys teasing Oliver.*] So what sort of boys are they?
Robbie: Big, they—
B.D.: Big boys, and should they say that to Oliver Button?
Robbie: Yes.
B.D.: They should? [*surprised*] . . . [*Reads about boys writing "Oliver Button is a Sissy" on the school wall.*] How does Oliver feel?
Robbie: Sad.
B.D.: He's very sad, isn't he? So should the boys have written that on the wall?
Robbie: [*Nods.*]
B.D.: They should? [*surprised*] Why should they have written that on the wall?
Robbie: Because he, because he's a sissy doing tap dancing. (Davies, 1989a, pp. 27–28)

As Robbie struggles to achieve himself as masculine, he understands as legitimate the work that others engage in to maintain the gender order of which he himself is becoming part. He has as yet no discourse that allows him to see the gender order as anything other than an obligatory structure into which each person must fit, no matter what the pain. Children, too, can be given access to an understanding of the constitutive force of language and of the possibility of refusing the old subject positions of old discourses. They, too, can participate in the creative constitution of new discourses that open up new possibilities, that encourage the multiplicity that comes so easily to them, and that adults generally work so hard to constrain.

Conclusion

The "wholeness" of *La Jeune Née,* the newly born woman, lies in *jouissance,* which implies not just sexual ecstasy, but has political and economic overtones, implying "total access, total participation as well as total ecstasy" (Cixous and Clément, 1986, p. 165), such totality being incompatible with being the other to male within the male/female dualism. *J'ouis sens* is derived from the sound of *jouissance*: I hear meaning. These are the meanings that must be spoken/written into existence outside the male/female dualism, outside the binary logics inside of which the male/female dualism takes its meaning.

Cixous implores women to write, to seize and make words their own, to take risks, to rid themselves of fear and caution, to open up the possibility of loving with all of themselves, not desiring the other through lack, but desiring all of the other with all of oneself. That *one* self is not a simple sum of her/his parts but a multiplication of difference. The profound complexity of the third space is knowing oneself as a woman, and in that knowing breaking the bonds of words and images and metaphors that have held one inside the male/female dualism, that have made one a woman in phallogocentric terms. Cixous (1981, p. 250) says:

> To write. An act which will not only "realize" the decensored relation of woman to her sexuality, to her womanly being, giving her access to her native strength; it will give her back her goods, her pleasures, her organs, her immense bodily territories which have been kept under seal; it will tear her away from the superegoized structure in which she has always occupied the place reserved for the guilty (guilty of everything, guilty at every turn: for having desires, for not having any; for being frigid, for being "too hot"; for not being both at once; for being too motherly and not enough; for having children and for not having any; for nursing and for not nursing . . .)—tear her away by means of this research, this job of analysis and illumination, this

emancipation of the marvellous text of her self that she must urgently learn to speak.

We do not know what we can speak/write into existence until we've done it, since even those imaginary worlds through which we conjure up a possibility different from this world are discursively produced. We need to write and speak utopias, we need to rewrite the past and the present, we need to write and speak all of our selves, not just our minds but our bodies, to *imagine* who we might be if we were not constituted within the bonds of the male/female dualism. According to Clément (1986), the newly born woman must transcend the heresies of history and the history of hysteria; she must fly/flee into a new heaven and a new earth of her own invention.

~

In this chapter I have assumed women's power to eclipse the conditions of their own emergence. Like Butler I want to continue to use a concept of agency that suggests the possibility of going beyond the conditions of our subjection. In the following chapter I turn my analytic gaze on the concept of agency to see in what way we might legitimately continue to use it in a poststructuralist framework.

Notes

1. Sex, once understood as physical (meaning natural), and gender, once understood as social, are no longer able to be divided in this way, since the physical can be shown to be largely socially constructed. I have thus merged sex and gender into the one term "sex/gender" to make it clear there is nothing in the gender order that is unequivocally "natural" (Connell, 1987; Davies, 1989b; Butler, 1990).

2. Kristeva's term for those who take up this third desiring space is the *avant garde*. It is in others' elaborations of this tier, or generation, or space, that it has been equated with a poststructuralist position.

4 ~ The concept of agency

W ITHIN THE HUMANIST DISCOURSES that predominate in the social sciences, agency is synonymous with being a person. It is used inter-
changeably with such concepts as freedom, autonomy, rationality, and moral
authority. In this chapter I will explore some of the problems with this model
and the possibility of unhooking the concept of agency from humanist versions of the person and redefining it in feminist poststructuralist terms.
There are a number of fundamental differences between the way the concept
of being a person is theorized by humanists as opposed to the way it is theorized by poststructuralists.

In poststructuralist theory, which is developed in large part in contrast to
humanist theory, "the subject itself is the effect of a production, caught in
the mutually constitutive web of social practices, discourses and subjectivity;
its reality is the tissue of social relations" (Henriques et al., 1984, p. 117). In
this model our existence as persons has no fundamental essence; we can
only ever speak ourselves or be spoken into existence within the terms of
available discourses. We are thus multiple rather than unitary beings, and
our patterns of desire that we took to be fundamental indicators of our
essential selves (such as the desire for freedom or autonomy or moral rightness) signify both the discourses and the subject positions made available
within them, through which we have been constituted and through which
we have constituted ourselves (Walkerdine and Lucey, 1989). From a poststructuralist perspective, agency cannot be any of the things that it is
assumed to be in humanist thought. What it might be I will come to after
elaborating the humanist position and some of the problems with it.

In the humanist or individualistic model of the person, agency is, by definition, a feature of each sane, adult human being. Those who are generally
not constituted as agentic, such as women, children, natives (to borrow a
term from Trinh Minh-ha), and the insane are, by definition within that
model, not fully human. Agency, for them, is the exception rather than the
rule. As well, agency assumes an agonistic relationship between the self and
other and between the self and society (Carbaugh, 1988/89). Individuals are
conceived as being in relation to something external to themselves called
"society," which acts forcefully upon them and against which they can pit
themselves. Closely linked to this understanding is the celebration of the

This chapter was originally published by the journal *Social Analysis* 30 in 1991.

individual who is seen to stand out from the collective. Modern history is thus the story of celebrated individuals and of their impact on the world. Modern stories, similarly, are about heroes who engage in specific tasks and conquer the difficulties that the world puts in their way. The people about whom these stories are told are not understood as beings discursively produced by their times, but as the individuals writ large that we might each imagine becoming as we struggle towards our own individual personhood.

Embedded within the dominant humanist discourses (through which, in part, we are spoken and speak ourselves into existence) is an understanding that being a person entails an obligation to take oneself up as a knowable, recognizable identity, who "speaks for themselves," and who accepts responsibility for their actions. Such responsibility is understood as resting on a moral base and entailing personal commitment to the moral position implied in their choices. It is this discursive placing of responsibility that makes us, in a legalistic sense, agents by default. Furthermore, it is the rational aspects of the individual self that are understood to be in control of this process. These elements of the humanist position are summarized on the next page and contrasted with poststructuralist thinking on what it means to be a person.

Benson (1990) elaborates the humanist idea of agency as rational control of oneself with the emotional nonrational being defined as not-self. He points out how problematic this is insofar as it is essentially a masculinist and elitist definition. What is assumed, he points out, is that the choices this "rational self" will make are those that are approved of by those who are squarely located in and powerfully positioned within the dominant discourses. The necessary agreement and approval that makes the act in question definable as a rational one must be given by those who have access to the same value system and the same forms of reasoning and who would concur with the "free" choice that has been made. What these definitions of agency neglect, according to Benson, is making explicit their masculine and elite nature insofar as they do not acknowledge or recognize the normative interactive nature of agency. Rather, they see agentic acts as purely individual acts. Benson suggests that by seeing how agency is constituted, marginal members of society can cease blaming themselves for not being agentic and can challenge the dominant discourses (which constitute them as non-agentic). They can do so through such processes as consciousness raising, in which they develop a critical awareness of "normative domains." Benson does not hold out much hope for the effect of this process, however, because he recognizes that critical consciousness will not necessarily give one access to the normative competencies and positioning necessary to be agentic.

One reason for Benson's rather negative conclusion is that he does not question the legitimacy of his original definition of agency as control, with the rational controlling the irrational and emotional. This unquestioned

The Concept of Person in Humanist and Poststructuralist Theories

Humanism	Poststructuralism
1. Any sane, adult individual *has identity*. This identity is continuous, unified, rational, and coherent. Language is used to learn about and later to describe or analyze the self and the real world in which it finds itself. The language itself is a transparent tool for the achievement of such descriptions and analyses. Conscious, rational, linguistic processes are used by the individual to dominate those irrational, emotional aspects of self that might otherwise disrupt claims to *coherent adult identity*.	1. The experience of being a person is captured in the notion of *subjectivity*. Subjectivity is constituted through those *discourses* in which the person is being positioned at any one point in time, both through their own and others' acts of speaking/writing. One discourse that contradicts another does not undo one's constitution in terms of the original discourse. One's subjectivity is *therefore necessarily contradictory*. It is also to some extent outside of or larger than those aspects of being that come under rational or conscious control.
2. The *choices* that the individual makes are based on rational thought and are thus coherent choices that signal the coherence and rationality of the individual. People who do not make choices on this basis are regarded as faulty or lacking in some essential aspect of their humanness.	2. The *"choices"* that the individual makes may be based on rational analysis, but desire may subvert rationality. *Desires are integral to the various discourses through which each person is constituted* and are not necessarily amenable to change through rational analysis. Subject positions that individuals may take up are made available through a variety of discourses. One subject position, more often made available to white middle-class males than to others, is of the agentic person who can make rational choices and act upon them.
3. The individual is socialized in the first instance by the collective. Society's norms and values are internalized and become part of the individual. The individual is understood, nonetheless, within the terms of the individual/collective dualism—that is, *the essence of the individual is precisely that which the collective is not*. To "follow the crowd" is to have failed to establish one's own identity. To stand apart and to assert oneself in the face of the crowd is to have had particular success as an individual.	3. The concepts of the individual and the collective are not understood in terms of a dualism. *The individual is constituted through the discourses of a number of collectives as is the collective itself.* One can only ever be what the various discourses make possible, and one's being shifts with the various discourses through which one is spoken into existence. The individual or heroic "I" is understood as a discursive construction, not stemming from the particular characteristics of that person but from the subject position made available to her/him.
4. Continuity of identity is understood as arising from early socialization and internalization of a coherent set of values.	4. Fragmentation, contradiction, and discontinuity, rather than continuity of identity, are the focus. Investment in particular discourses, embodiment, and the material force of the discourses through both the individuals and social structures of which we are constituted are the major explanations of the experience of continuity.
5. Stories are versions of events that occur in the real world. An important distinction that is made by competent agentic adults is between "true" and fictional stories.	5. Stories are the means by which events are interpreted, made tellable, or even livable. All stories are understood as fictions, such fictions providing the substance of lived reality.

boundary between the rational and irrational is closely allied with the boundary between the conscious and the unconscious. Both can also be seen as masculinist humanist constructions, to the extent that the celebration of rationality and linear forms of thought requires the exclusion from conscious consideration of all those elements that do not fit the dominant concept of the unitary, rational human individual. (It also gives greater value to thought or argument that is constrained within a single form of discourse since that favors the probability of internal consistency.) The conscious and the unconscious mind are set up in opposition to each other—a dualism similar (and not unrelated) to the male/female dualism, in which there are two hierarchical opposites that take their meaning in relation to each other and cannot exist without the other, but are in constant battle with each other. The conscious mind is superior yet always at risk of being undermined by the unconscious. This dualism needs to be deconstructed along with the male/female dualism and all the other dualisms that are fundamental to modern Western discourse if we are to move beyond the limitations and strictures of humanist and masculinist versions of the world.

As I discussed in the previous chapter, Cixous (1981) claims that women are better placed than men to move into forms of being not constrained or contained by the male/female dualism. It is also possible that they are better placed to deconstruct the conscious/unconscious dualism. Because of their otherness to masculinity, women are also constituted as other to conscious/rational thought, despite the fact that they have had access to this form of thought through their schooling. They are thus competent within the terms of, but not wholly identified with, conscious, rational thought, and they are able to include in the range of their considerations the emotions, feelings, and other "irrational" elements of their being that have been relegated to the unconscious by men (these being made oppositional to "good" thought, to masculinity, and to rational decision making). The willingness of women to tap those elements of their being that men have made, by definition, untappable, at least by the conscious mind, is a major source of the irritation that many men feel with women and is often used as a source of justification for women's marginalization in the public world. From a masculinist perspective, women's take-up of elements that are not regarded as includable in good, rational thought is incomprehensible. Once the boundaries between conscious and unconscious thought are recognized as boundaries both constructed around and constitutive of problematic humanist versions of the person, however, then women's disregard for these boundaries becomes a strength to be tapped in the deconstruction of the dualisms that are constitutive features of modern discourse.

In answer to Benson, then, by allowing oneself to be aware of the contradictions, of the discursive constitution of the self as contradictory (by claiming rather than disowning the unconscious and the "irrational" elements of subjectivity), one may have access to other ways of knowing and to powerful ways of being that are not the result of normative judgment from within the dominant discourses made by those positioned as agentic within them.

A further problematic aspect of the normative nature of agency that Benson argues is that moral rightness is defined by those with power and then used by them to judge as lacking all those who do not share those definitions or have access to those discourses. Frye points out that assumptions of moral rightness are generally equated with moral authority, and thus the authority to tell others what to do, thereby positioning those others as people lacking moral rightness or authority. She points out it is white middle-class males who generally have access to moral authority, though white middle-class females may gain it if sponsored by a male, in which case, she says, "One's rightness is not really one's own, in this case, but it is one's sponsor's rightness" (Frye, 1990, p. 134). More important, the imposition of white middle-class values on others who are not white and/or middle class is morally questionable. Being "good"—something desired by many women (that desire being fundamental to the cultural narratives through which femaleness is constituted)—is almost inevitably classist and/or racist. Lugones (1990, p. 140) discusses the bind in which women of color find themselves in considering these issues:

> So racism has several implications for agency. Among them I will mention the difficulty of forming intentions that are not formed in the mind of the racist; the difficulty of carrying out one's intentions within hostile meaning systems, some of which do not even countenance such intentions; the difficulty of trusting the success of one's intentions (given that some of the time, "success" just may really amount to not being taken seriously).

Smith (1987) provides the metaphor of the ball game to illustrate the way in which women *as women* are discursively constituted as *nonagents*. For our purposes here, along with women we include all those who are neither white, nor middle class, nor adult, nor "sane." Smith (p. 32) says:

> It is like a game in which there are more presences than players. Some are engaged in tossing a ball between them; others are consigned to the role of audience and supporter, who pick up the ball if it is dropped and pass it back to the players. They support, facilitate, encourage but their action does not become part of the play.

It is interesting to look at Smith's metaphor from a feminist poststructuralist perspective in which the game itself could be reconstituted through addressing such questions as the following: Who defines this as *the* game? Through which discourse(s) is it constituted? Who is granted an authoritative position within that discourse? If this is a discourse that is fundamental to the maintenance of the male/female dualism then how can it be resisted? Can we undo the game from within by drawing attention to elements of it that are susceptible to change? Can we counterpose another discourse against it that will highlight its masculinist nature, that will inhibit those who are given agentic subject positions within it and empower those who are oppressed by it? What patterns of desire are generated through this discourse/game that are likely to hold women into their oppressed position within it, despite their access to alternative discourses or to discourses of resistance? How are these patterns of desire held in place? Can we develop alternative metaphors and images and storylines to counteract the impact of this discourse?

In a poststructuralist analysis, agency is no longer central to the analysis of Smith's game. Choices are understood as more akin to "forced choices," since the subject's positioning within particular discourses makes the "chosen" line of action the only possible action, not because there are no other lines of action but because one has been subjectively constituted through one's placement within that discourse to *want* that line of action. By making clear the way in which a person is subjected by discourse, poststructuralist theory shows how agency is fundamentally illusory. However, it opens up another possibility, related to the idea of the speaking/writing subject who can use some of the understandings of poststructuralist theory itself to regain another kind of agency. The speaking/writing subject can move within and between discourses, can see precisely how they subject her, can use the terms of one discourse to counteract, modify, refuse, or go beyond the other, both in terms of her own experienced subjectivity and in the way in which she speaks in relation to the subjectivities of others.

A central question then becomes, in what sense am "I" spoken into existence through these discursive practices? What is the "I" that is thus spoken, that is the active agent of modern theory? Is it just a fragmented, discontinuous series of positionings through which we simply become that which various discourses make possible, or do we each in some sense take control of the "I" and the words through which it is spoken into existence?

Bakhtin (1981, p. 342) argues that language is spoken not only *as if it were* one's own—but in speaking it is taken on *as* one's own. One's words inevitably carry the accretions of others' past usages but are not recitations—rather, they are the available fabric with which each person "does" being a member of the various collectives in which they participate in their own particular way. Ricoeur (1979, p. 98) makes a similar point in his analysis of meaningful action as text:

What we have said . . . invites us rather to think of the sense of the text as an injunction starting from the text, as a new way of looking at things, as an injunction to think in a certain manner.

. . . The text speaks of a possible world and of a possible way of orienting within it. The dimensions of this world are properly opened up by, disclosed by, the text.

. . . That which we make our own—*Aneignung* in German—that which we appropriate, is not a foreign experience, but the power of disclosing a world which constitutes the reference of the text.

The words that become one's own, the positions that these words make it possible to take up, form a base from which individual persons speak *and* the world that is spoken about. It is both the case that being an individual involves the appropriation of the words of the collectives of which one is a member, and that that collective appropriates the individual at the moment that the individual speaks.

Henriques et al. (1984, p. 3) capture this dual sense of appropriation—of simultaneously appropriating and being appropriated—when they say they "use 'subjectivity' to refer to individuality and self-awareness—the condition of being subject—but understanding in this usage that subjects are dynamic and multiple, always positioned in relation to particular discourses and practices and produced by these—the condition of being subject." They point out that the French word for subject holds active subjectivity and being subjected together more readily than does the English. In English the subject is generally understood as the speaking, active person (though it is also the passive object of experiments). It is through the verb, to subject, that we can grasp the second meaning contained within poststructuralist ideas of subjectivity.

Trinh (1989, p. 35), in contrast, adopts an extreme position when she says that the "me" can disappear while the "I" is merely a linguistic requirement in the construction of texts, those texts being a result of our common way of handling texts:

Why view these aspects of an individual which we imply in the term "writer" or "author" as projections of an isolated self and not of our common way of handling texts? For writing, like a game that defies its own rules, is an ongoing practice that may be said to be concerned, not with inserting a "me" into language, but of creating an opening where the "me" disappears while "I" endlessly come and go, as the nature of language requires. To confer an Author on the text closes the writing.

In the context of literary discourse, in which textual meanings are often tied to the established myths about the Author, this is an important point to make. But in practice we do speak ourselves into existence and thus become objects of our own and others' discursive practices, albeit shifting, always unfolding, relatively fragmented objects.

Just as there are multiple readings of any text, so there are multiple readings of ourselves. We are constituted through multiple discourses at any one point in time. While we may regard a move we make as correct within one game or discourse, it may equally be dangerous within another. A feminist desire to be recognized, or to have access to storylines with female protagonists or female heroes, may, from a feminist poststructuralist perspective, be seen as a desire made relevant in an outmoded discourse. But it may be inevitable that we go on reading ourselves and being read within the terms of such outmoded discourse, at least to some extent, since access to a new discourse does not undo or overrule the other as we supposed it did when we were ruled by the principles of logocentric thought. Not only will others continue to constitute us in terms of humanist discourse, but we cannot easily shed the patterns of desire, nor the interpretive frameworks that we took up as our own in learning to understand and use humanist discourses, which we did, not just as social scientists, but as participants in the everyday world. Similarly, we are constituted as gendered through complex metaphors and storylines that constitute (and through which we constitute) ourselves as embodied and desiring beings.

In the following autobiographical episode from *Lake Wobegon Days* (Keillor, 1986, pp. 230–31) Keillor illustrates the dual process of being subjected and actively taking up the terms of subjection. He describes boys being subjected as footballers, and he and his friends becoming the feminine other, and then goes on to describe a later heroic moment in which he reclaimed his own dominant heroic masculinity. This episode illustrates the way in which the mobilization of a dominant discourse by someone who is positioned and positions himself as having unquestionable authority can undercut the subject's capacity to maintain the discourse within which he had previously been taking himself up:

> In August, Coach Magendanz gets in his Chevy wagon and drives around recruiting Leonards for football season. . . . "You coming out for football?" he says to a big boy he's found mowing hay in a ditch. The boy is not sure. "You queer?" Coach asks. "If you are, I don't want you." The boy thinks he may after all. . . . In football, it's kill or be killed, and he needs some killers. "There is an animal in you and I intend to bring it out," he tells the team on the first day of practice. . . . He picks out two big boys to stand up and face each other. "Okay Stuart," he says, "rip his shirt off." Stuart advances. "You gonna let him rip your shirt off, Stupid?" Coach yells. Stupid isn't. They go at it in the hot sun, fooling around at first but then the animal in them comes out. They grunt and pant, rolling in the dirt, getting wrist holds, leg holds, ripping each other's

shirts off, until Coach calls them off. "That's football," he says. "Any pansies in the bunch can get up and leave right now."

Some of us who are more sophisticated drift by the practice field on our bikes. . . . We wave to them, on our way to go swimming. He looks at us and we don't hear what he says to them; he says, "I gueth they can't take their eyeth off you guyth." We hear about it later, and far from being sophisticated, we are filled with terror. All those afternoons we went skinny-dipping, the curiosity about what each other looked like—is something terrible going on? Are we that way? Perhaps we are, otherwise why are we so uncertain about girls? We don't talk about this. But each of us knows that he is not quite right. Once, at the river, Jim made his pecker talk, moving its tiny lips as he said, "Hi, my name's Pete. I live in my pants." Now it doesn't seem funny at all. *If it's not wrong, why were we worried that someone would come along and see?* . . .

When I was fourteen, [my Uncle Earl] came up to bat one hot July afternoon in the Father-Son softball game and looked at me playing third base and pointed his bat at me. I crouched; my mouth was dry and my heart pounded. He waited for a low pitch and drove it straight down the baseline—a blazing swing, a white blur, a burst of chalk dust—I dove to my right just as the ball nicked a pebble—it bounced up and struck me in the throat, stopping my breath, and caromed straight up in the air about fifteen or sixty-five feet. Blinded by tears, I hit the ground face first, getting a mouthful of gravel, but recovered in time to catch the ball and, kneeling, got off a sharp throw in the vicinity of first which caught him by a stride. I was unable to speak for twenty minutes. That play was some proof that I was alright. Everyone saw it and said it was great; even guys who didn't like me had to say that because it was.

At first, riding on their bikes, the boys feel "sophisticated." the "animal" nature of football bears no relation to them. But the coach, who occupies an authoritative position in male American culture, disrupts that sense of themselves by discursively constituting their nonengagement in football as indicators of homosexuality: "I gueth they just can't take their eyeth off you guyth." He thus positions them as "queer," as watching not from a superior viewpoint but with illegitimate and laughable sexual desire. Since it is possible for the boys on their bikes to find evidence to support either discourse, they find themselves threatened by the "evidence" in their practices that supports the coach's discourse. They do not have available to them the possibility of refusing the discourse, not only because they do not question the authority of the coach but because they can find elements of their experience that might count as "proof" that the coach is right. Further, they don't have access to an alternative authoritative discourse about homosexuality. They are thus faced with the uncomfortable possibility that the coach's discourse is legitimate. If it is legitimate, then they have to find proof within the terms of the coach's discourse to "prove" their heterosexuality. By engaging in an act that can only be construed as heroic within the coach's terms, Keillor describes himself getting himself off the hook in one sense (he is definitely not "queer"), but caught on another, because he has been subjected by the coach's discourse with its attendant assumptions and practices of hegemonic masculinity. He has been constituted as male within the terms of the coach's discourse and he has made these part of his own subjectivity. He is subjected and made subject. He *chooses* to "prove himself" in the coach's terms and from within the subjectivity made available to him within those terms.

Whether or not Keillor's action is viewed as agentic ultimately rests on the discourse through which it is constituted on each separate occasion it is spoken about and the position within that discourse that one is in when considering the act in question. A liberal humanist interpretation of this passage would inevitably see Keillor *becoming* a successful male through this experience, using terms such as self-actualization or individuation to describe the process. A poststructuralist analysis would be more likely to suggest that his subjectivity, at the time of the softball game, was constituted through and in terms of his access to the subject position of hegemonic male. Through the ways in which he chooses to tell this story in later tellings it can become any number of things. He may invest himself in the moment of catching the ball in such a way that it becomes his proof of his own prowess in hegemonic forms of masculinity. Or he may (as he does) retrieve his earlier perception of himself and show how he was forced into an amusing moment of hegemonic heroism through the contradictory discourses through which masculinity is constituted.

Theorizing the person as constituted afresh through each discursive act appears to contradict the sense we have of ourselves as continuous. That sense of continuity is created in part through the humanist discourses in which we come to understand ourselves as having an essential self. This "essential self" is achieved through a number of other features of the discourses through which each person is constituted. These include such things as:

- consistent positioning within a frequently used discourse, that positioning then appearing, both to the person and to others, to emanate from an "essential self";

- the use of a socially available repertoire of storylines through which the elements of a person's existence can be tied together into a repeated "meaningful" continuity;

- the inscription in one's body (of the physical body and also the body of desire) of the ways of being that are appropriate to the subject positions usually taken up (cf. Grosz, 1990); and

- consistent features of all discourses, such as the male/female dualism, that are achieved and thus experienced as natural features of persons when they are actually derived from the structure of discourse itself (cf. Butler, 1990).

The effects of being positioned differently within new discourses can bring about observable dramatic personal changes. But there can also be deep resistance to such changes, even when at a rational or intellectual level the change is regarded as desirable. There can be, as discussed in Chapter 3, a clash between feminist belief and feminine practice, the adherence to the latter being a source of frustration to the feminist in question. One source of such a clash can be accounted for in the third feature listed above, the idea of bodily inscription. If one's body has learned to interact with the world in certain ways, then these ways may need more than access to a new discursive practice to change them. Or the means of translating an idea into everyday practice may not easily be achieved, one's life-practice-as-usual or life as the practical expression of old familiar discourses always coming more readily to hand.

Recently I attended a seminar given by a PhD student of mine on the resistance to the ordination of women in the Anglican church in Australia. She put up on the overhead projector a number of quotes both from the Bible and from the resisters. One strong source of resistance was the horror some people felt at the presence of a *woman's body* in the sanctuary, that space near the altar where only the (male) priest should go. My conscious attention during the seminar was directed towards her presentation of the ideas that she and I had talked through, and to the audience response. Towards the end of the seminar I became aware of a sense of my own body that I had forgotten I ever had, in particular a sense that there was something wrong with my body, that wrongness being associated with my female genitals. I had grown up with this feeling, though I had not been able to articulate it until I had access to feminist discourse. The awareness that I now had was therefore more vivid than it had been in childhood, and far from regarding it as essential to myself or of being female, as I once had, I could see it as fundamental to the religious discourse that was part of the data being presented in the seminar. It was nevertheless an extraordinary feeling to be reinscribed, even momentarily, as wrong, deformed, and as in error seeking to position myself as a legitimate member of the public world. In part the reinscription was achieved through reading the substantive claims of the people quoted in the data, but it was also achieved through the structural feature of the language used, in which the masculine pronoun was the generic, constituting male as norm and woman as other.

The reason Keillor and I were vulnerable in each of these moments is in large part attributable to the way in which the male/female dualism is fundamental to all discourses. In his case, he was compelled to constitute himself as not other to male, that is as heroic and agentic, and I was subjected to myself as other-to-male, myself as one, in this particular case, who would induce horror in people should I presume to position myself as a legitimate speaker in the public world, or even worse, in sanctified spaces reserved for those made in a male god's image. To be other than male, that is, opposite of heroic and being worthy of recognition, is to find myself shrinking away from public notice. The linguistic structure through which the male/female dualism is reconstituted in almost every act of speaking has a powerful determining effect on what is possible/thinkable. To think of agency while the male/female dualism is intact is to think, almost inevitably, in terms of a male, other-than-female, heroic individual who stands out from the crowd, whose life is the stuff of history. To conceive of agency once the male/female dualism begins to be troubled is to think of speaking subjects aware of the different ways in which they are made subject, who take up the act of *author*ship, of speaking and writing in ways that are disruptive of current discourses, that invert, invent, and break old bonds, that create new subject positions that do not take their meaning from their genitalia and what they have come to signify.

The model of the person being developed here is of an embodied speaker who at the same time constitutes and is constituted by the discursive practices of the collectives of which she or he is a member. Each person speaks from the positions made available within those collectives through the recognized discourses used by that collective, and has desires made relevant by those discourses. One of the features of feminist collectives is that they hold open the possibility and the ideal of crossing traditional boundaries and of coming to know, not only through the discourses of one's class and race of origin but through the discourses of classes and races of one's feminist colleagues, lovers, friends (de Lauretis, 1987). As individuals who speak, we *may* be heard as having *author*ity. Not authority in the sense of the one who claims and enforces knowledges, dictating to others what is "really" the case, but as a speaker who mobilizes existing discourse in new ways, inverting, inventing and breaking old patterns (Cixous, 1981). In a poststructuralist framework *author*ity or agency can be thought of as:

- the discursive constitution of a particular individual as having presence (rather than absence), as having access to a subject position in which they have the right to speak and be heard;

- the discursive constitution of that person as author of their own multiple meanings and desires (though only to the extent that the person has taken on as their own the discursive practices and attendant moral commitments of the collective(s) of which they are a member);

- a sense of oneself as one who can go beyond the given meaning in any one discourse and forge something new, through a combination of previously unrelated discourses, through the invention of words and concepts that capture a shift in consciousness that is beginning to occur, or through imagining not what *is*, but what *might be*. Of this possibility Irigaray (1985, p. 29) says, "One would have to listen with another ear, as if hearing an 'other meaning' always in the process of weaving itself, of embracing itself with words, but also of getting rid of words in order not to become fixed, congealed in them."

Such a definition can then inform our concept of agency, since an agent could well be defined as someone who was able to speak with *authority*. That ability would not derive from personal individual qualities, but would be a discursive positioning that they and others sometimes had access to. Feminist, poststructuralist *authority* would not be coercive and would not be located within dominant discourses except insofar as it persuaded them to change themselves, to become more multiple, flexible, and inclusive of different points of view. Poststructuralist theory turns the equation between rationality and agency on its head. In understanding the discursive construction of self one is *liberated from* the burden of a rationality that controls, dominates, and negates feeling, the concrete, and the real in favor of the abstract and a notion of the good (which is not only probably not one's own, but which is coercive and judgmental of those not powerfully located in dominant discourses). Agency is never freedom from discursive constitution of self but the capacity to recognize that constitution and to resist, subvert, and change the discourses themselves through which one is being constituted. It is the freedom to recognize multiple readings such that no discursive practice, or positioning within it by powerful others, can capture and control one's identity. And agency is never autonomy in the sense of being an individual standing outside social structure and process. Autonomy becomes instead the recognition that power and force presume subcultural counter-power and counter-force and that such subcultures can create new life-forms, which disrupt the hegemonic forms, even potentially replacing them (Ryan, 1989).

Conclusion

To be a feminist, or a feminist theorist, is to engage in the very act of choosing to speak, of discovering the possibility of *authority*, of using that speaking, that *authority*, to bring about fundamental changes in the possible ways of being that are available to oneself and others. To this extent a feminist is a protagonist inside the storylines she is living out. In refusing patriarchal, logocentric discourse—and the positionings made available to women within them—she achieves more than the act of speaking from within another discourse. She may fundamentally change some aspects of patriarchal discourse itself. She cannot do this on her own, since her words must become a way of speaking that those constituted within the terms of patriarchal discourse take up as their own. Though one can never escape structure, structures are constituted through practice and practice can always be turned against structure (Connell, 1987, p. 95).

Agency is spoken into existence at any one moment. It is fragmented, transitory, a discursive position that can be occupied within one discourse simultaneously with its nonoccupation in another. Within current ways of speaking it is a readily attainable positioning for some and an almost inaccessible positioning for others. Individuals who are positioned on the female side of the male/female dualism or on the negative side of any other dualism such as black/white, child/adult, mad/sane are rarely heard as legitimate speakers, are rarely positioned as having agency. The language that embeds such dualisms needs breaking up. The dualisms that constitute the lived reality of those who are placed on the negative side need uncoupling, respeaking. Words need reworking. Authority needs to be reconceptualized as *author*ity, with emphasis on authorship, the capacity to speak/write and be heard, to have voice, to articulate meanings from within the collective discourses and beyond them. This capacity does not stem from the essence of the person in question but from the positions available to them within the discourses through which they take up their being. Each author needs to be understood not as one who uses language to articulate some objective truth but as one who "is shaken by, traversed by, vulnerable to, other views, other writings" as one who "does not edit or censor to reach a preset goal when a conceptual problem or tangle is encountered; [but] attempts to move through in the medium of language, not to a truth already known, but to a truth yet to be discovered" (Nye, 1989, speaking of Cixous, pp. 238–39).

~

In the next chapter on women's subjectivity and feminist stories I play with and further explore that shaking and traversing and the possibility of going beyond what is already known.

5 ~ Women's subjectivity and feminist stories

I N THIS CHAPTER I DRAW TOGETHER reflections on the nature of women's subjectivity and the relation of that subjectivity to lived and told stories, and to feminist stories in particular. This is not a linear story about women's subjectivity that has as its central organizing feature a rationally planned and executed argument. Rather, this story is a mixture of rational argument, emotion, and lived bodily experience, intertwining what we think of as fantasy and reality, and embracing contradictory positions. Although each fragment is illuminating in and of itself, together they represent the complex interplay of a woman's subjectivity and feminist stories.

I draw on episodes from my own life and on feminist stories and images to illustrate the ways in which poststructuralist theory can inform our thinking about the experience of being female, feminine, and feminist. Feminist post-structuralist writers such as Cixous (1981, 1986) have argued for a multiple wholeness for women that incorporates both sides of the current oppositional and hierarchical dualisms through which femininity and masculinity are currently constructed. In this chapter I explore the formation of female/feminist subjectivity and in particular the place of story in that formation. This exploration is aimed at locating the ways in which feminist subjectivity is impeded or enhanced through the taking up of particular storylines as one's own and examining the changes taking place in lived and told feminist narratives as we find ways to constitute ourselves outside the male/female dualism.

Women

In what sense do I speak here of "women" and their subjectivity? I am not speaking in an essentialist sense about all people who happen to have female genitals but about the discursive category female/woman and the experience of being discursively constituted as one who belongs in that category. Feminist discussions often fall apart on the terms *woman* and *man*, because it is assumed that the speaker is saying "all women" or "all men" and anyone can instantly think of exceptions to the apparently universalistic statement that

This chapter was originally published in the book *Investigating Subjectivity,* edited by Carolyn Ellis and Michael Flaherty and published by Sage in 1992.

is being made. When I talk about the experience of being "a woman," I refer to the experience of being assigned to the category female, of being discursively, interactively, and structurally *positioned* as such, and of taking up as one's own those discourses through which femaleness is constituted.

The concept of positioning is central to an understanding of the way in which people are constituted through and in the terms of existing discourses. The discourses through which the subject position "woman" is constituted are multiple and contradictory. In striving to successfully constitute herself within her allocated gender category, each woman takes on the desires made relevant within those contradictory discourses.

The contradictory knowing that inevitably results can debilitate women in a world in which humanist discourses are hegemonic and dictate that contradictory knowing is flawed knowing. Their contradictory subjectivity is called irrational, lacking in direction; their knowledge is intuitive, incomprehensible, or wrong. Alternatively, women who discover poststructuralist discourse can find in each moment of contradiction a clearer comprehension of their own fractured and fragmented female subjectivity (Haug et al., 1987). They do so through recognizing the constitutive force of discourse and the means by which it inscribes in the body and emotions of the constituted subject. Once they refuse to peel off or ignore that which does not fit a linear, noncontradictory storyline and see how they are positioned within the various constitutive discourses, they can begin to refuse some of those positionings and along with them the particular discourse in which they are embedded. The issue ceases to be the vulnerability of the essential female self attempting to do that which history says she cannot do. It becomes instead the analysis of discursive practices and the finding of ways to collectively resist the constitution of woman inside the male/female dualism. This chapter is, in part, an exploration of that possibility.

Although masculinity also is forged out of contradictory discourses, men have tended to cope differently. Among the many discursive strategies they use to deal with their lived contradictions is the distinction between self (the "I," which is unitary and private) and roles (the various "me's," which are multiple and public). Using this model, it is possible to act in contradictory ways without the coherence of oneself or one's rationality being called in question.

Although women/feminists have used the conceptual apparatus of *role,* they have often been uncomfortable with it as a means for interpreting behavior and have sought alternatives (Edwards, 1983; Henriques et al., 1984; Stanley and Wise, 1983; Walkerdine, 1981). One source of that disease is that as long as "I" and "me" are separated out, then the personal and private "I" can legitimate any social world in which the various public "me's" play out the different and contradictory roles that "society" demands. By making a strong boundary between the real "I" and the role-playing "me" it is not only possible to maintain an illusion of an essential, unitary, non-contradictory self, but the "me's" in this model need not be taken on as part of that essential self and therefore do not necessarily come within the gambit of personal moral responsibility.

In rejecting the division between the public and the private as a legitimate and meaningful division, feminists have owned their various "me's" and not reserved these or distinguished them from some other, independent, illusory "real" self. Perhaps for this very reason, feminists have found contradictory moral imperatives much more personally troubling as they try to integrate the unintegratable into one unified, rational, whole "me/I," struggling at the same time with the overriding imperative that links being a woman with being good.

The distinction between positioning and "role" is an important one in the feminist poststructuralist framework. Role is something that is simply taken on and cast off, with a "backstage" person taking up and casting off a variety of roles. One also moves through multiple positionings in any one day or even in any one conversation. Positions are discursively and interactively constituted and so are open to shifts and changes as the discourse shifts or as one's positioning within or in relation to that discourse shifts. Who I am potentially shifts with each speaking, each moment of being positioned within this or that discourse in this or that way. At the same time, personal histories of being positioned in particular ways and of interpreting events through and in terms of familiar storylines, concepts, and images that one takes up as one's own effectively constitute the me-ness of me separate from others. To the extent that *one takes oneself up* in terms of these familiar positionings and storylines, to the extent that one's moral commitments, patterns of desire, and ways of knowing and being are constituted through these positionings and storylines, then *they are inseparable from the subjectivity of that person.* This involves not just a psychosocial becoming but a physical reality in terms of the way one learns to walk and to sit and to move generally, even down to the detail of how one breathes (Haug et al., 1987; Wex, 1979).

Poststructuralist theory thus opens up the possibility of seeing the self as continually constituted through multiple and contradictory discourses that one takes up as one's own in becoming a *speaking subject.* One can develop strategies for maintaining an illusion of a coherent unitary self through conceptualizing what we do in terms of "roles" or through denial of contradiction, or one can examine the very processes and discourses through which the constitution of self takes place. Through locating the source of the contradiction in the available discourses, it is possible to examine the contradictory elements of one's subjectivity without guilt or anxiety and yet with a sense of moral responsibility. Dealing with contradiction within this model can enable one to take up the possibility of acting within the terms of one discourse rather than another at any one point in time, depending on its relevance, the values of its products, how one is positioned within it, and so on. Or it can facilitate a decision to refuse a discourse, or to refuse the positioning made available within that discourse. It can also facilitate an understanding of the collective and discursive nature of such refusals and of the ways in which one might begin to generate alternative practices.

Probably the most deep-seated taking up of oneself relates to sexuality, and in particular choices as to hetero- or homosexuality. These are so deeply felt that they are invariably experienced as and assumed to be "natural." Yet as we come to understand the extensive constitutive work that goes into creating and sustaining "correctly" gendered selves it is becoming clear that there is little about it that is unequivocally natural (Butler, 1990; Connell, 1987). The questioning continues as feminist biologists begin the massive task of deconstructing that which the biological fraternity assumed in their research to be the "natural order" of human/animal life (Davies, 1989a, 1989b; Rogers, 1988; Sayers, 1986). Butler (1990, pp. 22–23) points out that the "institution of a compulsory and naturalized heterosexuality requires and regulates gender as a binary relation." The differentiation of the masculine term from the feminine term, she says, is accomplished through the "practices of heterosexual desire." The more successfully we constitute ourselves as male and female, especially in terms of heterosexual desire, the more we believe that the product of that constitutive work is natural (p. 139):

> Gender is, thus, a construction that regularly conceals its genesis; the tacit collective agreement to perform, produce, and sustain discrete and polar genders as cultural fictions is obscured by the credibility of those productions—and the punishments that attend not agreeing to believe in them; the construction "compels" our belief in its necessity and naturalness.

Through taking up as her own the discourses through which femaleness is constituted, each woman becomes at the same time a speaking subject and one who is subjected or determined by those discourses. That subjection is generally invisible because it appears not only to be natural, as Butler points out, but also to be what women *want*, a result of free choice (Walkerdine and Lucey, 1989). But women's desires are the result of bodily inscription, and of metaphors and storylines that catch them up in ways of being/desiring from which they have no escape unless they can reinscribe, discover new storylines, invert, invent, and break the bounds of old structures and old discourses.

Poststructuralism offers those who have never been recognized as having the subject status that men have had a way of recognizing the means by which they have been subjected, made object, deprived of agency, and inscribed with patterns of desire that hold that oppressive cultural pattern in place. In what follows I tell some fragments of my own experience, fragments that bear little relation to the person I currently experience myself to be. Yet the person I was in these fragments is no longer alien and strange, nor even foolish, because I can now see how I was being discursively constituted. I was simply working within the constraints of available discourses to constitute myself as comprehensible, knowable, worthwhile.

Some of my own contradictions

I was born in the mid-1940s in a country town in Australia. In the early fifties in Australia there was much talk of war, of the possibility of future wars, and of the necessity of bravely defending our shores. Being a person of value and of note seemed to be understood solely in terms of the heroism of military action, itself expressed in terms of a willingness to die for principles of freedom through taking active measures to defend our country against the "yellow peril" in the north and the dreaded threat of "communism." There was also talk of the pain that the women who waited at home experienced. There was nothing they could do to help and no way they could know what was "really happening" out there in those foreign places. Their position, the antithesis of heroism, was one of unknowing, patience, privation, hardship, and namelessness. There was a disquiet about the position of women and also a strong emphasis on the value of "womanly" qualities and the importance of the woman in the home (Friedan, 1963).

Taylor (1990, p. 1) talks of women in Australia in the forties who contested this construction. She says that,

in their attempts to assume the burden of citizenship, they challenged the discourse of politics and war which from the time of the Greeks through to more recent times allocated to the male the task of *armed civic virtue* and the role of the warrior; and to the female, the archetypal roles of sacrificial mother and/or ministering angel as well as the task of weeping, mourning and, at times, goading to action.

But such contestations are not any part of my conscious remembering of my childhood. I understood as fact that women could not be soldiers, but I rejected the position of the women who hopelessly waited. I understood my rejection of that position as something original that I had thought of for myself, not recognizing that it was part of an emerging discourse being made available to me in some of the talk that was going on around me. My search for what else I might be, other than someone who waited, I understood and remembered as a private, individual reflection on the nature of existence. I remember thinking that the closest I could come to doing something of worth was to be a nurse and care for the heroes who actively fought for that which was of value.

But, as I listened to my parents talk, this "solution" began to seem untenable. In the eyes of my father, nurses were sexually available, and therefore not, according to my mother, in the category of woman who could be respected or accorded any value other than sexual. Sexually available women could not be wives. While my father prized sexually active women and spent his life bemoaning the fact that my mother was not one of these, the way he talked about them made them seem laughable, sleazy, and disposable. Two of my aunties were nurses and these two aunties were not married. This was held up, in subtle ways, as proof of their failure to be the right kind of women.

Somehow one had to juggle the contradictory imperatives to be a good woman, to be sexually active without negating one's goodness, and to find at the same time some form of heroism not incompatible with either of these. I read voraciously, and I repeatedly came across the pattern of female heroism that combined a fear of not being worthy or loved with an extraordinary capacity to sacrifice oneself for others and to care for them, particularly if they were damaged or imperfect in some way. These characteristics I took up as my own, along with the relevant patterns of desire.

At the age of twenty I met a man who had been temporarily released from jail to attend university. Following a record of violence and living outside the law, he was struggling to make something of his life "within the law." He was both talented and very much harmed by his time in jail. Who better than I to help him? I married him and the prison released him into my care. At the age of twenty, carrying his child, I took on the hopeless task of making good the lack of care that he had suffered throughout his life, of loving him well enough to heal his damaged being, of sacrificing myself to the task of supporting his genius. Needless to say, I failed. The storylines through which I made sense of my life were nonsense in the face of the damage done by the prison system, and no amount of feminine care and self-sacrifice could restore the damage. For five years the three children and I were battered prisoners in the "domestic haven" that I had learned to want (Davies, 1989c).

The romantic storylines through which I interpreted my life are some of the lived realities of the male/female dualism and they work to hold that dualism in place. Within the terms of these romantic storylines the desire to correctly constitute oneself as woman entails taking up as one's own oppressive subject positions that no one would ever rationally choose. The "choice" arises from one's history in the world as female/woman/feminine. The recognition of the storyline as problematic and the possibility of refusing it and of generating alternatives come from the poststructuralist analysis of it.

Women's subjectivity

> Is "humanity," as a reality and as an idea, a point of departure—or a point of arrival? (Gramsci, 1957, p. 79)

Within poststructuralist thought, the person (and the idea of what it means to be a person) is collectively and discursively constituted. The collectivity of women with their shared experiences and emotions—their female subjectivity—is made possible because as "women" they are spoken into existence through the same collective set of images, metaphors, and storylines as other women. Individuals are made distinguishable from the total collective through assignment to gender category and then through naming. The assignment of gender places the child in relation to others in particular ways. The naming, done in relation to the gender assignment, both marks and heightens the assignment, making the child's gender always available in any speaking to or of the child. Its family name further positions the child in relation to families—usually as belonging in one and not in the others.

Each child faces the task of performatively and conceptually distinguishing the "me" from the "not-me." The me (or I) is understood and performed as having an inner quality as well as surface appearances and historical/geographical locations. The inner quality, what we have come to know as *desire,* is not just a physical inner quality but a psychic quality. The desires of the individual are what characterize "this person" to her- or himself. This is how I "know" myself. The "real me" is the psychic me, the desiring being. Although those desires are demonstrably discursively produced and thus collective in nature, they are "taken on" by each individual as their inner core.

According to Althusser (1971), subject status is guaranteed even prior to birth and is guaranteed through the familial ideological pattern of each person's origin. In the majority of cultures this is done through the name of the father:

> Everyone knows how much and in what way an unborn child is expected. Which amounts to saying, very prosaically, if we agree to drop the "sentiment", i.e., the forms of family ideology (paternal/maternal/conjugal/fraternal) in which the unborn child is expected: it is certain in advance that it will bear its Father's Name, and will therefore have an identity and be irreplaceable. (Althusser, 1971, p. 176)

Cunningham (1989) uses this quote from Althusser as a point of departure for his analysis of the autobiography of a black male slave, Douglass, who, in contrast to what Althusser takes as normative, did not know his father's name. Douglass describes himself thus:

I was born in Tuckahoe, near Hillsborough, and about twelve miles from Eas-
ton in Talbot County, Maryland. I have no accurate knowledge of my age, never
having seen any accurate record containing it.

My father was a white man. He was admitted to be such by all I ever heard
speak of my parentage. The opinion was also whispered that my master was my
father; but of the correctness of this opinion, I know nothing; the means of
knowing was withheld from me. (pp. 47–48)

Douglass's description of himself begins with the place of his birth. The
absence of the father comes after that location of himself in place. As Cohen
and Somerville (1990) have shown in their work on Australian Aboriginal
identity, place can be a fundamental defining feature of persons. Cunningham misses the significance of this, primarily because he is caught up in the
Freudian storyline as *the* storyline through which individuals' stories must
be told.

He makes a great deal of the nonsubject status of Douglass as slave, which
he relates to the lack of the father's name. He relates the concept of *being a
subject* to having an "ego" and ties this to the oedipal drama acted out in relation to the master. That Douglass's mother gave him a name is considered by
Cunningham not to reduce the impact of no name from the father, despite
Althusser's careful disclaimers and his final statement that it is into particular kinds of families that one is born: "Before its birth, the child is always-
already a subject in and by the specific familial ideological configurations in
which it is 'expected' once it has been conceived." To an extent, however,
Douglass also shares Cunningham's and Althusser's prioritizing of the name
of the father insofar as he defines himself in terms of the absence of the
father and of not knowing his father's name (and, therefore, presumably his
own, even though his mother had given him a name). From a feminist poststructuralist position this cannot be read as depriving him of subject status
but, instead, as Douglass constituting himself within the terms of that same
patriarchal discourse that dictates that the father, whether by his presence or
his absence, is a crucial defining feature of who the male child is.

Cunningham compares the slaves' plight with that of women and talks of
the alternative to subject status being that of object. In doing so he is fundamentally misunderstanding what it means to *be subject*, at least in poststructuralist terms. He takes his idea of subject, at least in part (though probably
unintentionally), from the liberal humanist, masculinist (and middle-class)
tradition in which humanity is assumed to be intricately connected to
agency, which means the power to choose and to make decisions in relation
to one's own life. In this mode, the opposite of subject is object—that is,
someone who is deprived of agency and who is subjected to the agentic acts
of others. But the meaning of subject in poststructuralist writing takes its

meaning in contrast to this liberal humanist idea of the subject. The various discourses in which one participates, or in terms of which one gains a voice or becomes a speaking subject, also are the means by which one is spoken into existence (even prior to one's birth) *as subject*. These discourses subject each person to the limitations, the ideologies, the subject positions made available within them. We become, not what we have learned to call our true essential selves, but that which the various discourses in which we participate define as or make thinkable as a self, or a true self. The mistake that we make, according to Althusser (1971), is to see ourselves as authors of those selves, rather than to recognize that discourses are the means by which individuals are taken over by various "state apparatuses." Our selves and our human nature are not the causes of what we do but the products of the discourses through which we speak and are spoken into existence:

> The fundamental innovation of Marxism into the science of politics and history is the proof that there does not exist an abstract, fixed and immutable "human nature". (Gramsci, 1957, p. 140)

> What we had thought of as human nature is, rather, a regulatory fiction through which people can be ordered and located in hierarchies. (Butler, 1990, p. 24)

In the experience of most women, the name of the father is granted unproblematically (though only temporarily, as something to be replaced by another man's name). The name of the father is no guarantee of subject (i.e., non-object) status in Cunningham's terms, since recognition of herself as one with a right to be heard as a speaking subject is never guaranteed. The father's name is more like a sign of temporary ownership, not a sign that this is someone with a life of her own. It is in fact her sex that names her, that subjects her to the storylines in which not only is she object but her desire and others' desire for her is organized in terms of that object status. The naming and the storylines, through which that naming is made to make sense, are not an external clothing that can be cast aside but become the very subjectivity through which each woman knows herself:

> "Sex", the category compels "sex", the social configuration of bodies, through what Wittig calls a coerced contract. Hence the category of "sex" is a name that enslaves. Language "casts sheaves of reality on the social body" but these sheaves are not easily discarded. She continues: "stamping it and violently shaping it". (Butler, 1990, p. 115)

Cixous (1986) has been of central importance in the task of reworking old discourses and generating new ones. In much of her writing she explicitly challenges elements of existing discourses. One of her strategies is to tell the old stories again, but in such a way that the unacceptable features of them become painfully clear. Two "perfectly" passive feminine beings who represent the archetypal object of male desire are Sleeping Beauty and Snow White. Their passivity is so perfect it is akin to death. Cixous (1986, p. 66) writes of Sleeping Beauty and her sisters,

> *Once upon a time... once... and once again*
>
> Beauties slept in their woods waiting for princes to come and wake them up. In their beds, in their glass coffins, in their childhood forests like dead women. Beautiful but passive; hence desirable: all mystery emanates from them. It is men who like to play dolls. As we have known since Pygmalion. . . . She sleeps, she is intact, eternal, absolutely powerless. He has no doubt that she has been waiting for him forever.
>
> The secret of her beauty kept for him: she has the perfection of something finished. Or not begun. However she is breathing. Just enough life—and not too much. Then he will kiss her. So that when she opens her eyes she will see only him; *him*; him in place of everything, all him.

Although this telling of Cixous's is in part through the eyes of male desire, it is also a telling that reveals the absence of woman to herself inside the romantic storyline. It shows the way in which woman's subjectivity, her desire, her sense of herself is inscribed in body and mind in terms of this storyline and probably will be until such time as she can both understand it and its fascination for her and write a better one. As long as this is her only or predominant storyline, she will struggle to achieve the correct degree of submissiveness in order to be sufficiently desirable to be positioned within that story. To be in no story is inconceivable. The achievement of oneself as woman within the romantic storyline is a taking up of herself as female subject within the terms of the discourses through which she is spoken and speaks herself into existence.

Feminist writers such as Wittig have begun the task of creating new storylines with new images and metaphors that position women quite differently. In the following passage Wittig (1969, p. 16) brings Snow White, in her coffin, to a different kind of life:

> The gypsy women have a mummified corpse which they bring out when it is not raining, because of the smell of the body which is not quite dry. They expose it to the sun in its box. The dead woman is clothed in a long tunic of green velvet, covered with white embroidery and gilded ornaments. They have hung little bells on her neck, on her sleeves. They have put medallions in her hair. When they take hold of the box to bring it out the dead woman begins to tinkle everywhere. Every now and then someone goes out on to the

three steps that lead up to the caravan to look at the clouds. When the sky is obscured two of them set about shutting the lid of the box and carrying it inside.

In this image of Wittig's, Snow White is undoubtedly a corpse. But she has more beauty, even more life with its tinkling bells, than Cixous's woman, who is the object of male desire. It is the women in this story who care for this faintly absurd object and decorate it beautifully, not so that one would long to be positioned as it is, but, with tenderness and amusement, they care for its eternal being. The woman in the coffin prompts an active reading of the absurdity of being the totally passive, deathlike "love-object," suggesting not simply angry rejection for its deathlike positioning, but an amused recognition, and thus a possibility of movement beyond.

Women's subjectivity and feminist stories

The task of generating feminist storylines that have the power to disrupt and displace the old is extraordinarily complex. This is so for a number of reasons. First, new stories are always at risk of being interpreted in terms of the old. Second, our patterns of desire are not easily disrupted, in particular to the extent that they are defined as signifying one's essential self. Third, the function of story in holding the existing order in place has not yet been fully understood. Poststructuralist and postmodern stories function in a number of ways to break up old patterns (Hite, 1989). Farmer (1990, p. 4) cites Zweig on the topic of the attitudes to story that are beginning to emerge with postmodern consciousness:

> Recently, however, we have begun to expect another pleasure from the stories we read. The spectacle of life's hidden form emerging from the vagaries of experience no longer warms our hearts. On the contrary, it chills us just a little, as if the form were a prison, and the novel's end-informed story the evidence for a failure of spirit. What [we want] are disruptive moments, flashes of illuminating intensity. It is not the end which is important, but the episode; not the form, of which the end is the final clarity, as when a sculptor unveils a statue, but the illumination itself, unruly and momentary, not casting a new light over what has been lived, but compressing life itself into its absoluteness, and bursting.

Much feminist writing has precisely that quality of "bursting open" the holding power of old storylines. This is not just an angry fracturing and breaking of unwanted images and positionings—though it is also that—but the bursting forth of the bud from the death of the female winter:

then the day came
when the risk to remain
tight in a bud
was more painful
than the risk it took
to blossom
(a quote from Anaïs Nin on my physiotherapist's wall)

Because fantasy is understood as somehow integral to childhood, children are not immediately introduced to the fact/fantasy dualism. Adults go to some lengths to acquaint children with the world of fantasy via stories, and they collude in persuading children to believe stories that they themselves do not believe to be true. In deep contradiction with this particular practice, however, we require of children's tellings of their own experience a sharp dividing line to be drawn between "real" and "pretend" that they then take up as an important way of categorizing their tellings. Real is legitimate and has force, while pretend is dismissible and positively evil if it is not clearly marked "pretend."

Learning to separate the two clearly is a signal that one has become adult and is a legitimate and worthy person within the terms of modern thought. But the task of separation is never complete because it is a discursively produced difference that needs constant work to achieve it as an observable difference. The fabrication of difference is manifest in those practices in which what a person "really" thinks and feels becomes a matter that counselors and friends help him or her "discover." Such attitudes and processes are fundamental to the construction of gendered unitary, noncontradictory humanist persons who constitute themselves as having a real, discoverable essence in clear distinction to the social and discursive forces that surround and produce them.

In this humanist/modernist model, stories serve a number of functions. They can be an escape from the real world, or they can be didactic, teaching morals to the reader, or inspiring the reader to better things. But they can also be seen by modernist moralists as dangerous and misleading, filling the "hearts and minds" of readers with *mistaken* versions of reality that they then confuse with real life. The specific danger of the romantic storyline within a modernist understanding of story is women's tendency to construe the most ordinary and flawed of men as "their prince." Such construal can lead to inappropriate commitment, passion, and inevitable disillusion when the cracks in the supposed reality start to reveal themselves. "Am I *really* in love?" was the anguished question we often asked each other in those days of clear separation between fact and fantasy, and we assumed that if the answer was yes, the storyline would unfold correctly with its inevitable happy ending of fulfillment and domestic bliss. If the prince was an ogre, no matter, her real love would turn him into a prince. In this model it was my capacity to "really" love that was at fault, or else it was a flawed choice on my part, having not recognized an ogre that could not be changed into a prince. Either way, I am guilty.

From a poststructuralist perspective, there is no longer any "real" lived story. Stories we observe, hear, and read, both lived and imaginary, form a stock of imaginary storylines through which life choices can be made. The choices I make in any current moment will depend on the storyline I take myself to be living out. If I think I am in the romantic narrative, which requires "the prince," the people with whom I choose to play out this story will be more or less able to live out the prince as I understand it, depending on whether they take themselves to be inside the romantic storyline, what their particular version of the romantic storyline is, and their ability and/or willingness to live out that which is necessary in my storyline for them to continue to be read as prince.

In poststructuralist terms, to get out of the romantic narrative, to escape its confines, I don't need to catch myself mistakenly reading someone as prince when he is not. Instead, I need to understand the story itself, how it draws me in, and how others position me within its terms. I need as well to imagine new storylines in which the problems inherent in the existing narrative are eliminated and in which the positionings available to me are not destructive in the way that the romantic narrative is. In such an interpretation it is not the individual woman who is at fault in mistakenly living out a fantasy instead of a reality or for living it incorrectly. It is the culture that has destructive narratives through which identity and desire are organized. The task becomes one of looking for and generating new storylines. It is also one of discovering what the "hooks" are in the images and metaphors of the old storylines that can draw individual women in against their better judgment. In this postmodern version of the relation between lived and imaginary narratives, imagined stories are a valuable resource since they may hold a key to disrupting and decentering old discourses and narratives—to unstitching and fraying the patterns of desire that are held within them.

Readings of a feminist story

The following story was written for me by my youngest son, Daniel. I had been complaining to him about the impossibility of ever writing a feminist story since there is always the possibility of a conservative reading in which the story is understood as confirming the status quo. After examining several of my attempts and discussing the problems I found with them, and after discussing the ways in which the images I drew on carried unwanted baggage in his readings of them, Daniel took up the challenge of writing a feminist story.

The following is his story. He was twenty at the time of writing it. It is interesting that he starts with a character who, like him, is the third child and who, like him, had a cruel father whom she never knew.

Vuthsanya

Now it so happened that a third child was born to King Rian, and was not a male. This angered the King greatly, for it had been foretold that his third child was to be gifted with great powers of knowledge and skill, especially in battle.

The King himself was a mighty ruler and man of renown. He was so angered by the birth of his third daughter that he refused to speak to her or even to see her. Her name was Vuthsanya and she only ever looked upon her father's face once. She had eyes of the blackest of black and secrets the darkest of dark.

On her twelfth birthday she left the castle and the Kingdom carrying only the clothes on her back. The King soon learned of her departure, yet he sent no search party and shed no tear. Many others did, for Vuthsanya was well liked by the people although none could claim to know her well.

The next ten years were the coldest and hardest years the Kingdom had ever known. Crops failed, sickness plagued the land, the sun seldom shone, and the King was growing old. It was then that a terrible creature came to the land. He was Teg-Mushrak, one of the ancient tormentors, who took delight in death and destruction. In looks he was something like a giant ogre, yet much more repulsive. Mushrak terrorised the Kingdom for months without rest. Rian had sent many brave knights out to finish him, but none came back.

In frustration and dismay the King sent forth a demand for Mushrak to meet him on the field of battle. This challenge was accepted gleefully by the blood-hungry tormentor. So it was set. In one week, on Mid-Winter's Eve, the two should meet in battle on the Felion Plains below the cliffs of Aspirion.

The day quickly came and the King went to meet his doom. The people were frightened and would not come out of their houses. Children wept and the men felt shamed for there was nothing they could do but hope.

Rian reached the plains and there was Mushrak, picking his teeth with the splintered thigh bone of a victim. He laughed and spat at Rian who was clad in bright armour, riding a white steed and carrying a long shining lance. "Prepare to meet your end!" yelled King Rian, as he charged towards the foul creature with blood in his eyes. But Rian was not the young warrior he once had been and Mushrak leapt aside with surprising speed and knocked Rian from his horse with a tremendous blow. The King fell to the ground and was dazed. He unsheathed his sword but Mushrak leaped in the air and dealt his head a mighty kick which rendered him unconscious, and at the ogre's mercy, of which there was none.

Mushrak was preparing to sink his teeth into his prize when he heard the beating of huge wings above him; he wheeled around and was dealt a sickening blow across the side of the head. Mushrak stumbled with blood pouring out of his face, saliva dribbling down his chin and gave a thunderous bellow of anger. He turned to face his foe, and his anger, as great as it was, gave way to a chuckle, and then a laugh. "A woman dares to attack Mushrak, the most powerful and wonderful creature in the land," he snorted. "I will teach you the folly of your ways!"

Vuthsanya was sitting astride a black Pegasus with her long sword drawn and no light shone from her eyes. She leapt from her mount with agility and stood to face Mushrak. She said nothing.

The giant ogre lunged towards Vuthsanya, but she nimbly ducked aside and slashed his side so that blood poured out like water.

This angered Mushrak beyond belief and he spun around, madly trying to claw at this arrogant pest. But he was no match for Vuthsanya. With two more blows, Mushrak was begging for mercy. The next blow split Teg-Mushrak's skull in two. He was dead and Vuthsanya stood tall and proud over her fallen foe.

Now King Rian awoke from his slumber and saw what had taken place and looked for the mighty warrior who had done this amazing deed, for he would most certainly be the King's new champion. But all he could see was a mighty black Pegasus flying off into the distance with a woman's figure astride. It seemed then to Rian that he knew who this was, though he could not say, or perhaps would not.

Rian rode home and the people rejoiced to see their King return. To this day people still tell the story of Rian's battle with Teg-Mushrak and how he split the monster's head in two and so saved the land. Only two people know what really happened that day, and so do you.

~

We can read this story conservatively, *with* the grain of patriarchy. In such a reading there are many features that appear to confirm the status quo:

- Fathers do not welcome or value daughters, particularly when their heart is set on a son capable of heroism;

- good daughters cope with such rejection with silence and with absence, since there is nothing they can say to undo such rejection;

- mothers are also silent and do nothing to question or reverse the plight of their daughters;

- even when the daughter is the exception to the rule and is capable of heroism, the father will not acknowledge such heroism, nor will the daughter ask him to do so.

But there is also much about the story that makes a different reading possible, a reading that runs against the grain of discourses that constitute women inside the male/female dualism. That alternative reading provides a critique of patriarchy and gives the reader an alternative storyline.

First, the father's belief in the inferiority of women is shown to be wrong. Girls *can* have powerful knowledge and be great warriors. ("It had been foretold that his third child was to be gifted with great powers of knowledge and skill, especially in battle.") Her knowledge and her strength are not only greater than his, but, perhaps more important, cannot be attributed to him. The powerful and all-rejecting father is shown to be dishonest, claiming her accomplishments as his own. His law rests on a shaky foundation that not only invites criticism but is recognizable as falsely depending on the unacknowledged support of women.

Second, the daughter reveals that his judgment is of no consequence to her. She can walk away from it and set up an alternative life in which she is clearly extraordinarily powerful. It is within her gift to save her father and his kingdom, which she does, but his recognition of this fact is of no consequence to her. This can be read as a profound negation of the word/the law/the power of the father. She thus has far greater moral stature than he since she does not hold grudges or seek revenge even when this would seem to be an entirely reasonable response.

There are some additional features of the story that involve the reader in reading against the conservative grain of the story. One of these is the ending in which the author invites the reader to position her- or himself as one who knows the truth, and thus as one who shares Vuthsanya's knowledge. The reader then stands with Vuthsanya against the power of the father. The story is told from the moral position of Vuthsanya but in an interestingly "unfeminine" way. The kinds of details that are normally revealed in the telling of women's lives are left completely untold. She is a genuine protagonist mixing some features of the male heroic position with some features of the heroine. As heroine she is, at the beginning, vulnerable in the way that heroines usually are. She is at risk of being rejected by a central male figure, in this case, the father. She has no safe domestic scene and is cast adrift, presumably with the task of finding a new one. But she turns this around. Her story becomes one that is more typical of the male hero. She is powerful, competent, and strong. The home base that she creates is not described, and, perhaps more important, nor is she (except for the blackness of her eyes, whose most prominent quality is what they hide). Nor is she the object of another's gaze, nor does she need anyone else to make her safe.

Since the story begins with the familiar scene of rejection, it has the power to "hook" a female reader who can connect with the subjectivity of

Vuthsanya and know her vulnerability. It maintains this connection in a number of ways. Vuthsanya remains caring in that she saves her father when he needs it and she does not confront or demand in an "unfeminine" way. Her warriorlike skills are the most significant point of departure in her character from current accepted forms of femaleness/femininity.

Vuthsanya is thus not a character who asks us to negate our femininity but one who says that, along with feminine qualities and even when positioned as inferior/female, women can be heroic and can thus exist outside and independent of the male/female dualism. She can exist not as *woman* but as a multiple being who incorporates and reconstitutes that which was previously understood as essential to either masculinity or femininity.

Conclusion

Who we are, our subjectivity, is spoken into existence in every utterance, not just in the sense that others speak us into existence and impose unwanted structures on us, as much early feminist writing presumed, but in each moment of speaking and being we each reinvent ourselves inside the male/female dualism, socially, psychically, and physically. The lived and imaginary narratives that we generate in our attempt to speak into existence a different way of being outside the male/female dualism need to achieve several contradictory purposes. We need stories that are elaborations of existing stories that mark their problematic nature. We need not only to see the problems in rational, didactic terms (though we need that, too) but to see freshly the images and metaphors and storylines we have become and to learn to read them against the grain. The desire to read them against the grain does not simply come with knowing what those alternative readings are, however, since the old storylines, through which old discourses are lived out, inevitably compete for our attention. Any reading against the grain implies a detailed knowledge of the grain itself. And who we have taken ourselves to be in the past and in much of the present is known precisely in terms of that which we are trying to undo. As Hollway (1984, p. 260) says of new discourses and new practices:

> Changes don't automatically eradicate what went before—neither in structure nor in the way that practices, powers and meanings have been produced historically. Consciousness-changing is not accomplished by new discourses replacing old ones. It is accomplished as a result of the contradictions in our positionings, desires and practices—and thus in our subjectivities—which result from the coexistence of the old and the new. Every relation and every practice to some extent articulates such contradictions and therefore is a site of potential change as much as it is a site of reproduction.

One of the major contributions of feminist fictional writing has been to invent new images for readings outside the male/female dualism. In the following passage from Wittig (1969, p. 19), a new image of female genitals is created that uses as the grain-to-write-against the old attitudes of shame and the related averted female gaze. The contradictory image that she creates is one in which female genitals are celebrated, not as objects of the male gaze, nor as signifiers that exclude women from the sacred or from power, but as signifiers of a power of mythic proportions:

> The women say that they expose their genitals so that the sun may be reflected therein as a mirror. They say that they retain its brilliance. They say that the pubic hair is like a spider's web that captures the rays. They are seen running with great strides. They are all illuminated at their centre, starting from the pubes of the hooded clitorides, the folded double labia. The glare they shed when they stand still and turn to face one makes the eye turn elsewhere, unable to stand the sight.

The multiple and contradictory nature of such rewriting of women as powerful cannot be incorporated in any one linear story. As I have tried here to draw together threads and fragments of my own life with images presented me by others to make a new kind of story that lends itself to multiple readings, so too our stories need to break their old shapes and burst forth into new ones. That bursting forth is not simply through the creation of images that others can be inspired by and follow. It is also a collective awareness of the power of speaking and writing, both to reconstitute ourselves in ways we do not wish within the male/female dualism and to create a succession of moments in which we know ourselves otherwise, as multiple and whole, encompassing in our beings both sides of any dualism, thus dismantling the dualisms themselves.

~

In the next chapter I turn to the analytic tasks begun in Chapter 4, "The concept of agency." Instead of the imaginary play that I have engaged in this chapter, I work with Rom Harré to tease out the conceptual possibilities of the concept of positioning. Because I am writing with Rom, we also draw on the concepts central to new paradigm psychology in this conceptual exploration and extension of poststructuralist thinking.

6 ~ Positioning: The discursive production of selves

T HE IDEA FOR THIS PAPER emerged out of a discussion between us about the problems inherent in the use of the concept of role in developing a social psychology of selfhood. We explore here the idea that the concept of "positioning" can be used to facilitate the thinking of linguistically oriented social analysts in ways that the use of the concept of role prevented. In particular, the new concept helps focus attention on dynamic aspects of encounters in contrast to the way in which the use of role serves to highlight static, formal, and ritualistic aspects. The view of language in which positioning is to be understood is the immanentist view expounded by Harris (1982), in which language exists only as concrete occasions of language in use. *La langue* is an intellectualizing myth—only *la parole* is psychologically and socially real. This position is developed in contrast to the linguistic tradition in which "syntax," "semantics," and "pragmatics" are used in a way that implies an abstract realm of causally potent entities shaping actual speech. In our analysis and our explanation, we draw on both concepts central to ethogenic, or new paradigm, psychology (Davies, 1982; Harré, 1979; Harré and Secord, 1973) and concepts central to poststructuralist theory (Davies, 1989a; Henriques et al., 1984; Potter and Wetherall, 1988; Weedon, 1987).

The immanentist account of orderly human productions

According to a long-established tradition, the orderliness of many human productions, for instance conversations, is a consequence of rules and conventions that exist independently of the productions. In some readings of the Chomskian school of linguistics, for example, transformational grammars are taken as preexisting their roles in actual psychological processes of language production. We shall call this kind of view "transcendentalism." In this chapter we take a contrary or "immanentist" view. We shall assume that rules are explicit formulations of the normative order that is immanent in concrete human productions, such as actual conversations between particular people on particular occasions. These formulations are themselves a special kind of

This chapter was written with Rom Harré and was originally published in the *Journal for the Theory of Social Behavior* 20(1) in 1990.

discourse having its own social purposes. According to the immanentist point of view there are only actual conversations, past and present. Similarities between various conversations are to be explained by reference only to whatever concretely has happened before, and to human memories of it, which form both the personal and cultural resources for speakers to draw upon in constructing the present moment. Though mnemonic devices such as books and manuals are often understood as evidence for preexisting knowledge structures independent of any speaker, these only have meaning to the extent that they are taken up by any speaker/hearer as encodings to be attended to. It is the actual conversations that have already occurred that are the archetypes of current conversations. We remember what we and others have said and done, what we believe or were told that they have said and done, where it was wrong and where it was right. In this view, grammar is not a potent psychological reality shaping syntactical forms. It is an aspect of a specialist conversation in which some people talk and write to and for each other about what other people say and write. In highly literate societies, instances of this kind of writing can be drawn upon as concrete exemplars of how to talk. We take an immanentist stance to all similar theories about the sources of patterned human productions, in particular towards social rule sets.

If we want to talk about "sexism" or "ageism" in the use of language, what we are talking about is the highlighting of certain past conversations as morally unacceptable exemplars for talking and writing now. The basis on which a cluster of past conversations can be deemed to be objectionable as exemplars for speaking now is not whether the speakers in the past or present intended their speaking to be derogatory of women or of the aged. Rather, it is because it can be shown that, as in the past, there can be negative, even if unintended, consequences of those ways of talking. "Position" will be offered here as the immanentist replacement for a clutch of transcendentalist concepts like "role."

Discourse, discursive practices, and the production of selves

We use the term "discursive practice" for all the ways in which people actively produce social and psychological realities. In this context a discourse is to be understood as an institutionalized use of language and language-like sign systems. Institutionalization can occur at the disciplinary, the political, the cultural, and the small group level. There can also be discourses that develop around a specific topic, such as gender or class. Discourses can compete with each other or they can create distinct and incompatible versions of reality. To know anything is to know in terms of one or more discourses. As Frazer (1990, p. 282) says of adolescent girls she interviewed: "Actors' understanding and experience of their social identity, the social world and their place in it, is discursively constructed. By this I mean that the girls' *experience* of gender, race, class, their personal-social identity, can only be expressed and understood through the categories and concepts available to them in discourse."

In this sense "discourse" plays a similar role in our social theory to that played by "conceptual scheme" in contemporary philosophy of science. It is that in terms of which phenomena are made determinate. An important distinction, though, between the two terms as we understand them is that conceptual schemes are static repertoires located primarily in the mind of each individual thinker or researcher almost as a personal possession, whereas discourse is a multifaceted public process through which meanings are progressively and dynamically achieved.

The constitutive force of each discursive practice lies in its provision of subject positions. A subject position incorporates both a conceptual repertoire and a location for persons within the structure of rights for those who use that repertoire. Once having taken up a particular position as one's own, a person inevitably sees the world from the vantage point of that position and in terms of the particular images, metaphors, storylines, and concepts that are made relevant within the particular discursive practices in which they are positioned. At least a possibility of notional choice is inevitably involved because there are many and contradictory discursive practices that each person could engage in. Among the products of discursive practices are the very persons who engage in them.

An individual emerges through the processes of social interaction, not as a relatively fixed end product, but as one who is constituted and reconstituted through the various discursive practices in which he or she participates. Accordingly, who one is is always an open question with a shifting answer depending upon the positions made available within one's own and others' discursive practices and within those practices, the stories through which we make sense of our own and others' lives. Stories are located within a number of different discourses and thus vary dramatically in terms of the language used, the concepts, issues, and moral judgments made relevant, and the subject positions made available within them. In this way poststructuralism shades into narratology.

We intend our development of the notion of positioning as a contribution to the understanding of personhood. The psychology of personhood has been bedeviled by the ambiguity of the concept of "self," a concept that has played a leading role in psychological discourses of personhood. Human beings are characterized both by continuous personal identity and by discontinuous personal diversity. It is one and the same person who is variously positioned in a conversation. Yet as variously positioned we may want to say that that very same person experiences and displays that aspect of self that is involved in the continuity of a multiplicity of selves. We believe that selfhood, or personal identity, is as much the product of discursive practices as are the multiple self-hoods we wish to investigate (Harré, 1983; Muhlhausler and Harré, 1990).

Our acquisition or development of our own sense of how the world is to be interpreted is from the perspective of who we take ourselves to be, and it involves, we claim, the following processes:

1. Learning of the categories that include some people and exclude others, e.g., male/female, father/daughter;

2. Participating in the various discursive practices through which meanings are allocated to those categories. These include the storylines through which different subject positions are elaborated;

3. Positioning of self in terms of the categories and storylines. This involves imaginatively positioning oneself as if one belongs in one category and not in the other (e.g., as girl and not boy, or good girl and not bad girl);

4. Recognition of oneself as having the characteristics that locate oneself as a member of various subclasses of (usually dichotomous) categories and not of others—i.e., the development of a sense of oneself as belonging in the world in certain ways and thus seeing the world from the perspective of one so positioned. This recognition entails an emotional commitment to the category membership and the development of a moral system organized around the belonging.

All four processes arise in relation to a theory of the self embodied in pronoun grammar in which persons understand themselves as historically continuous and unitary. The experiencing of contradictory positions as problematic, as something to be reconciled or remedied, stems from this general feature of the way being a person is done in our society. Within feminist poststructuralist theory the focus has been on the experience of contradictions as important sites for gaining an understanding of the discursive constitution of selves as gendered (Haug et al., 1987).

Smith (1988, p. xxxv) introduces the concept of positioning by distinguishing between "a person" as an individual agent and "the subject." By the latter he means "the series or conglomerate of positions, subject-positions, provisional and not necessarily indefeasible, in which a person is momentarily called by the discourses and the world he/she inhabits." In speaking and acting from a position people are bringing to the particular situation their history as a subjective being—that is, the history of one who has been in multiple positions and engaged in different forms of discourse. Self-reflection should make it obvious that such a being is not inevitably caught in the subject position that the particular narrative and the related discursive practices might seem to dictate.

Positioning, as we will use it, is the discursive process whereby selves are located in conversations as observably and subjectively coherent participants in jointly produced storylines. There can be interactive positioning in which what one person says positions another. And there can be reflexive positioning in which one positions oneself. However, it would be a mistake to assume that, in either case, positioning is necessarily intentional. One lives one's life in terms of one's ongoingly produced self, whoever might be responsible for its production.

Taking conversation as the starting point, we proceed by assuming that every conversation is a discussion of a topic and the telling of, whether explicitly or implicitly, one or more personal stories whose force is made determinate for the participants by that aspect of the local expressive order that they presume is in use and towards which they orient themselves. The same anecdote might seem boastful according to one expressive convention, but an expression of proper pride according to another. In either reading the anecdote becomes a fragment of autobiography. People will therefore be taken to organize conversations so that they display two modes of organization: the "logic" of the ostensible topic and the storylines that are embedded in fragments of the participants' autobiographies. Positions are identified in part by extracting the autobiographical aspects of a conversation in which it becomes possible to find out how each conversant conceives of themselves and of the other participants by seeing what position they take up and in what story, and how they are in turn positioned.

In telling a fragment of his or her autobiography a speaker assigns parts and characters in the episodes described, both to themselves and to other people, including those taking part in the conversation. In this respect the structure of an anecdote serving as a fragment of an autobiography is no different from a fairy tale or other work of narrative fiction. By giving people parts in a story, whether it be explicit or implicit, a speaker makes available a subject position that the other speaker in the normal course of events would take up. A person can thus be said to "have been positioned" by another speaker. The interconnection between positioning and the making determinate of the illocutionary force of speech acts may also involve the creation of other positionings by a second speaker. By treating a remark as, say, "condolence," in responding to that remark a second speaker positions themselves as, say, the bereaved. The first speaker may not have so intended what they said, that is, they may not wish to be positioned as one who would offer condolences on such an occasion.

When one speaker is said to position themselves and another in their talk, the following dimensions should be taken into account:

1. The words the speaker uses inevitably contain images and metaphors that both assume and invoke the ways of being that the participants take themselves to be involved in.

2. Participants may not be aware of their assumptions nor the power of the images to invoke particular ways of being and may simply regard their words as "the way one talks" on *this sort* of occasion. But the definition of the interaction being "of this sort," and therefore one in which one speaks in this way, is to have made it into this sort of occasion.

3. The way in which "this sort of occasion" is viewed by the participants may vary from one to another. Political and moral commitments, the sort of person one takes oneself to be, one's attitude to the other speakers, and the availability of alternative discourses to the one invoked by the initial speaker (and particularly of discourses that offer a critique of the one invoked by the initial speaker) are all implicated in how the utterance of the initial speaker will be heard. This is also the case for any subsequent utterances, though the assumption is usually made by participants in a conversation that utterances by speakers subsequent to the initial speaker will be from within the same discourse.

4. The positions created for oneself and the other are not part of a linear noncontradictory autobiography (as autobiographies usually are in their written form) but rather are the cumulative fragments of a lived autobiography.

5. The positions may be seen by one or other of the participants in terms of known "roles" (actual or metaphorical), or in terms of known characters in shared storylines, or they may be much more ephemeral and involve shifts in power, access or blocking of access to certain features of claimed or desired identity, and so on.

One way of grasping the concept of positioning as we wish to use it is to think of someone listening to or reading a story. There is the narrative, say *Anna Karenina,* which incorporates a braided development of several storylines. Each storyline is organized around various poles such as events, characters, and moral dilemmas. Our interest focuses on the cast of characters (for instance, Anna, Karenin, Vronsky, Levin, and Kitty). The storylines in the narrative describe fragments of lives. That there is a cast of characters from whose imagined points of view the events described in the narrative will be different opens up the possibility for multiple readings. Any reader may, for one reason or another, position themselves or be positioned with one or more of the characters within the story or as outside the story looking in. Such positionings may be created by how the reader perceives the narrator and/or author to be positioning them (as reader) or it may be created by the reader's perception of the characters themselves.

Transferring this conceptual system to our context of episodes of human interaction, we arrive at the following analogue: There is a conversation in which a braided development of several storylines is created. These are organized through conversation and around various poles, such as events, characters, and moral dilemmas. Cultural stereotypes such as nurse/patient, conductor/orchestra, mother/son may be called on as a resource. It is important to remember that these cultural resources may be understood differently by different people.

The illocutionary force of each speaker's contributions on concrete occasions of conversing can be expected to have the same multiplicity as that of the culturally available stereotypes as they are individually understood by *each* speaker. A conversation will be univocal only if the speakers each adopt complementary subject positions that are organized around a shared interpretation of the relevant conversational locations. Even then, the fact that the conversation is seen from the vantage point of the two different positions, however complementary they are, militates against any easy assumption of shared understanding.

One speaker can position others by adopting a storyline that incorporates a particular interpretation of cultural stereotypes to which the others are "invited" to conform, indeed are required to conform, if they are to continue to converse with the first speaker in such a way as to contribute to the storyline that person has opened up. Of course, they may not wish to do so for all sorts of reasons. Sometimes they may not contribute because they do not understand what the storyline is meant to be, or they may pursue their own storyline, quite blind to the storyline implicit in the first speaker's utterance, or as an attempt to resist. Or they may conform because they do not define themselves as having choice but feel angry or oppressed or affronted or some combination of these.

In our analysis of an actual conversation we will illustrate the importance of the insight that the same sentence can be used to perform several different speech acts. Which speech act it is will depend in part on which storyline speakers take to be in use. It follows that several conversations can be proceeding simultaneously. It also follows that one speaker may not have access to a conversation as created by another or others, even though he or she contributes some of the sentences that serve as pegs for the speech acts the others create (Pearce and Cronen, 1981). Our analysis indicates that any version of what people take to be a determinate speech act is always open to further negotiation as to what the actual act (if there is such a thing) is.

To illustrate the use of the concept of positioning for analyzing real conversations, we will describe a conversational event in which one speaker positioned another. What the positioning amounted to for each conversant will be shown to depend on the point of view from which the conversation is seen. Our example will draw on a case in which a single attribute, namely powerlessness, rather than a typified role model, was made salient. The main relevance of the concept of positioning for social psychology is that it serves to direct our attention to a process by which certain trains of consequences, intended or unintended, are set in motion. But these trains of consequences can be said to occur only if we give an account of how acts of positioning are made determinate for certain people. If we want to say that someone, say, A, has been positioned as powerless, we must be able to supply an account of how that position is taken up by A; that is, from whence does A's understanding or grasp of powerlessness derive? We can raise the same issue by asking what psychological assumptions cluster around the single attribute, in this case powerlessness, that the act of positioning has fastened on A. We shall call this an extension of the significance of the attitude.

For analytical purposes we propose two kinds of such extension:

- *Indexical extension.* For some people, in some situations, a position-imposed attribute is interpreted and the consequences of such positioning are taken up in terms of the indexical meanings developed through past experiences. "Powerlessness," for example, might be grasped in terms of what was felt on past occasions when a person took themselves to be powerless. With respect to this particular attribute, we have observed that women in industrial societies tend to make such extensions of the significance of the concept. The case is probably reversed for the attribute of powerfulness, in which women need to consult a typification, say mother, to know what it means. It follows that we would expect it to be the men among disadvantaged races or classes within such societies who take up the significance of being positioned as powerless indexically, that is, in light of their particular experiences of being robbed of choice or agency.

- *Typification extension.* In other cases the extension of the significance of an initial act of single-attribute positioning comes about through the association or embeddedness of that attribute within a culturally well-established cluster of attributes, called up by the positioning. In this case, we think, metaphorically, of a person scanning their past experience for a concrete occasion on which to build an interpretation of the position they have been assigned (whether they accept or reject it) until they encounter the record of a typified occasion, such as "nurse/patient."

In both forms of extension the storyline in which the person takes themselves to be embedded is a critical element in the process of establishing the meaning of the utterance in question.

Positioning compared to concepts used in the dramaturgical model

The classical dramaturgical model has focused on "role" as the determining basis of action. Though there have been attempts to recruit "improvised theater" to the models available for social psychology (Coppierters, 1981), it is the traditional drama that has served as the almost ubiquitous source model. In the dramaturgical model people are construed as actors with lines already written and their roles determined by the particular play in which they find themselves. Nor do they have much choice as to how to play these roles in any particular setting. They learned how to take up a particular role through observation of others in that role—the role models. "Positioning" and "subject position," in contrast, permit us to think we locate ourselves in conversations according to the storylines with which we are familiar and bring to those narratives our own subjective lived histories through which we have learned metaphors, characters, and plot. Consider, for example, the "role" of mother. Everyone "knows" what that is, and anyone finding themselves in that role, or in relation to someone in that role, knows the multiple expectations and obligations of care for children that it entails. There may be variations on the theme, such as "Jewish mother," but these are simply mothers who take up their role within a further set of constraints embedded in "Jewish culture." But everyone does not know each of our personal understandings and sets of emotions connected to our idea of mother, developed out of experience of our own mothers in the first instance. And those who develop their particular concept of mother in anticipation that they will one day be positioned as mother will do so differently from those who know that they will never be so positioned. The way we have been positioned and have positioned ourselves in relation to "mother," the narratives that we have lived out in relation to particular mothers, mean that we bring to each new encounter with someone positioned as mother a subjective history with its attendant emotions and beliefs *as well as* a knowledge of social structures (including roles) with their attendants rights, obligations, and expectations.

Any narrative that we collaboratively unfold with other people thus draws on a knowledge of social structures and the roles that are recognizably allocated to people within those structures. Social structures are coercive to the extent that to be recognizably and acceptably a person we must operate within their terms. The concept of a person that we bring to any action includes the knowledge of external structures and expectations, as well as the idea that we are responsible for our own lines; there are, however, multiple choices in relation not only to the possible lines that we can produce but to the form of the play itself. We are thus agent (producer/director) as well as author and player and the other participants co-author and co-produce the drama. We are also the multiple audiences that view any play and bring to it the multiple and often contradictory interpretations based on our own emotions, our own reading of the situation, and our own imaginative positioning of ourselves in the situation. Each of these will be mediated by our own subjective histories. Finally, as we will show, lived narratives can change direction and meaning in ways entirely surprising to the participants to such an extent that the metaphor of a prestructured play begins to lose plausibility as a viable image to explain what it is that we do in interaction with each other. If we are to come close to understanding how it is that people actually interact in everyday life, we need the metaphor of an unfolding narrative, in which we are constituted in one position or another within the course of one story, or even come to stand in multiple or contradictory positions, or in which we negotiate a new position by "refusing" the position that the opening rounds of a conversation have made available to us. With such a metaphor we can begin to explain what it means to "refuse" to accept the nature of the discourse through which a particular conversation takes place.

The closest one might come conceptually to role in our framework is subject position. A subject position is made available within a discourse. For example, in the discourse of romantic love there are two major complementary subject positions made available—the male hero or prince who has agency and who usually has some heroic task to perform, and the female heroine or princess who is usually a victim of circumstance and is reliant on her prince to save her from whatever it is that fate has done to her (Brownstein, 1984; Zipes, 1986). In everyday life, if two people are living out some version of the romantic love narrative, then they will position themselves and each other in the complementary subject positions made available within the discourse of romantic love. In other words, they will engage in the discursive practices through which romantic love is made into a lived narrative.

In Goffman's later works of 1974 and 1981, a different terminology appears as he shifts further from the dramaturgical model that animated his earlier work. An interest in the ubiquitous role of conversation in creating and maintaining social interaction led him to develop analytical concepts for understanding its properties. The earlier of his attempts was the idea of "frame." That this was not a well-thought-through concept can be seen in the following example. He begins by asserting that frames and schemata are the same thing:

> Frames vary in degree of organization. Some are neatly presentable as a system of entities, postulates and rules; others—indeed most others—appear to have no particular articulated shape. . . . (Goffman, 1974, p. 21)

The aim of the analyst is to isolate basic frameworks (primary frames) "for making sense out of events." The task is made difficult by the fact that while one thing may appear to be going on something else is happening; for example, an autobiographical anecdote may be intended as a joke, a wedding may be in a play, etc.

We can understand what is happening in a play by seeing that while the primary frame is being used by the audience to make sense of what the actors are doing, it must be understood "nonseriously," that is, as not having its usual consequences. Goffman called the use of a primary frame in play-going a "change of key"—the analogy with music was deliberate, suggesting a systematic transformation appropriate to a particular setting and antici-pated by the participants. Frames, like roles, are already given in a cultural system, and the occasions of their use, either in this key or that, are provided for socially, for example, by designating a certain arena as a playhouse. Thus the dynamic concept of positioning oneself in a discourse is not reducible to adopting a frame, though a frame may well come along with a position, nor is it reducible to a change of key, even though that one is positioned may be revealed as a key change.

Goffman's later idea of "footing" is more promising as an alternative to positioning. His metaphor is double. We gain or lose our footing in conver-sations, social groups, and so on, much as we gain or lose it on a muddy slope. In the second layer of metaphor, we speak from and can change our "footings" in conversations. Goffman's own account of his new notion is rather vague, since it relies on various other ideas, which themselves are not well defined. "Change of footing" is concerned with occasions when partici-pants' alignment, or set, or stance, or posture, or projected self is somehow at issue. "A change of footing implies a change in the alignment we take up to ourselves and to the others present as expressed in the way we manage the production and reception of an utterance" (Goffman, 1981, p. 128). So "alignment" emerges highlighted from these remarks. But one's hopes for clarity are dashed, since in the very next line Goffman ties footing back to his earlier and vague concept of frame: "A change in our footing is another way of talking about a change in our frame of events." But if we consult Goffman (1974) we find that a frame is simply a working set of definitions of the familiar Burkean kind, in which a scene, actor, and action are speci-fied in what is essentially a version of role analysis.

So let us return to footing. Goffman's analysis includes a conception of the speaker as fulfilling three speaking roles: that of "animator," he or she who speaks; that of "author," he or she who is responsible for the text; and that of "principal," he or she "whose position [i.e., where the speaker stands] is established by the words that are spoken, someone whose beliefs have been told, someone who is committed to what the words say" (Goffman, 1981,

p. 144). This is the basis of the production format of the utterance. On many occasions, animator, author, and principal are one and the same person.

Similar complexities attend the hearers. There is always a participation framework in place, including differentiations of "official recipients" of the speaker's talk from bystanders, eavesdroppers, and so on.

Staying now with alignment and relating it to production formats and participation frameworks, we still lack an account of what the key term means. Tannen tells us (personal communication) that alignment is a relational notion, but so far as we can judge, what alignments relate to are speakers' conceptions, linking the one adopted by the speaker with what sort of person the speaker takes the hearer to be. Similarly and sometimes reciprocally, there will be a pair of hearer's conceptions of the persons engaged in talk. An actual conversation will then realize, probably imperfectly, these beliefs as actual relations between participants. This could not be in sharper contrast to our conception of positioning, since it takes for granted that alignments exist prior to speaking and shape it, rather than that alignments are actual relations jointly produced in the very act of conversing. It should be clear that Goffman, even in his later work, did not escape the constraints of role theory. Frames and schemata are transcendent to action and stand to it as preexisting devices (or tools) employed by people to create conversations. For us, the whole of the "apparatus" must be immanent, reproduced moment by moment in conversational action and carried through time, not as abstract schemata, but as current understandings of past and present conversations.

A lived narrative and its analysis using the concept of positioning

The best way to recommend our proposal is to demonstrate its analytical power in a worked example.

In our story we have called ourselves Sano and Enfermada. Sano and Enfermada are, at the point the story begins, at a conference. It is a winter's day in a strange city and they are looking for a chemist's shop to try to buy some medicine for Enfermada. A subzero wind blows down the long street. Enfermada suggests they ask for directions rather than conducting a random search. Sano, as befits the one in good health, and accompanied by Enfermada, darts into shops to make inquiries. After some time it becomes clear that there is no such shop in the neighborhood and they agree to call a halt to their search. Sano then says, "I'm sorry to have dragged you all this way when you're not well." His choice of words surprises Enfermada, who replies, "You didn't drag me, I chose to come," occasioning some surprise in turn from Sano.

Sano and Enfermada offered separate glosses on this episode, whose differences are illustrative of the use of the concept of positioning and instructive in themselves since they reveal a third level of concepts beyond illocutionary force and positioning, namely moral orders. The subsequent debate between our protagonists ran as follows.

Sano protests that he feels responsible and Enfermada protests in return that she does not wish him to feel responsible since that places her in the position of one who is not responsible and, by implication, that she is one who is incapable of making decisions about her own well-being. They then debate whether one taking responsibility deprives the other of responsibility. For Sano the network of obligations is paramount. He is at first unable to grasp the idea that anyone could suppose that the fulfillment of a taken-for-granted obligation on the healthy to take charge of the care of the ill could be construed as a threat to some freedom that he finds mythical. Enfermada is determined to refuse Sano's claim of responsibility, since in her feminist framework it is both unacceptable for another to position her as merely an accessory to their actions, rather than someone who has agency in her own right, *and* for her to accept such a positioning. Her concern is only in part for the unintended subject position that his words have apparently invited her to step into. She believes that his capacity to formulate their activity in such a way may be indicative of a general attitude towards her (and to women in general) as marginal, as other than central actors in their own life stories. She knows that he does not wish or intend to marginalize women and so she draws attention to the subject position made available in his talk and refuses to step into it. But her protest positions Sano as sexist, a positioning that he in turn finds offensive. His inclination is therefore to reject Enfermada's gloss as an incorrect reading of his words. But this of course only makes sense in his moral order of interpersonal obligations, not in the feminist moral order. Both speakers are committed to a preexisting idea of themselves that they had prior to the interchange, Enfermada as a feminist and Sano as one who wishes to fulfill socially mandatory obligations. They are also both committed to their hearing of the interchange. Their protests are each aimed at sustaining these definitions and as such have strong emotional loading.

The episode went through a number of further cycles of reciprocal offense, too numerous to detail here. One of them involved Sano accusing Enfermada of working off a worst-interpretation principle, which he claims is characteristic of the kind of ultrasensitive response that feminists and members of minority groups engage in when responding to "fancied slights." Enfermada hears this as a claim that she is unnecessarily making life difficult for herself, alienating people (presumably including Sano) from her and her feminist views. This bothers Enfermada more than the original "apology" because she sees herself not only robbed of agency but as trivialized and silly, an objectionable member of a minority group who, if they behaved properly, could have equitable membership of society along with Sano. The whole point of her original protest was that his words robbed her of access to that equitable world whether he intended it or not. Until that point she had believed that his intentions were in fact good, which was why it was worth raising the issue. Now she sees that even knowing how upsetting it is to be so positioned in his narrative, his wish is to allocate all responsibility for inequitable treatment that she receives to her own personal style. And so the story went, with claims and counterclaims. The complexity, if not impossibility, of "refusing the discourse" became more and more apparent, as did the subjective commitment to implicit storylines with their implications for the moral characters of each of the participants.

Leaving aside for one moment the further cycles of offense that were generated around the original conversation, it is possible to render the episode in a symmetrical way and in terms of speech acts and illocutionary force as follows:

> *Us:* I'm sorry to have dragged you all this way when you are not well.
> *Ue:* You didn't drag me, I chose to come.

Let us all call these utterances or speech actions Us (Sano's utterance) and Ue (Enfermada's utterance) respectively. We shall use the symbols A(Us) and A(Ue) for the corresponding speech actions, which can be made determinate in the various storylines.

What speech acts have occurred? To answer this question we have first to identify the storylines of which the utterances of S and E (Us and Ue) are moments. Only relative to those storylines can the speech actions crystallize as relatively determinate speech acts.

> SS *S's storyline as perceived by S*: medical treatment with associated positions of S = nurse and E = patient. In this story A(Us) = commiseration.

> SE *S's storyline as perceived by E*: paternalism with associated positions of S = independent powerful man and E = dependent helpless woman. In this story A(Us) = condescension. Indexical offense S to E.

> EE *E's storyline as perceived by E*: joint adventure with associated positions of S and E as travelers in a foreign land. In this story A(Ue) is a reminder in relation to the storyline.

> ES *E's storyline as perceived by S*: feminist protest with associated positions of S = chauvinist pig and E = righteous suffragette. In this story A(Ue) = complaint. Indexical offense E to S.

There are several further points to be made in relation to this analysis. It shows the way in which two people can be living quite different narratives without realizing that they are doing so. In the absence of any protest on Enfermada's part, Sano need never have questioned how his position as caregiver would appear in the moral order of someone whose position was radically different from his. Without her particular reply he could not have realized that he could be heard as paternalistic. Her silence could only act as confirmation of his moral order.

Words themselves do not carry meaning. Sano's use of the apology format is ambiguous. When it is placed in the context of Enfermada's narrative it causes indexical offense. Similarly, her protest at being "made helpless" disturbs him since, in his story, it denies what he takes to be a ubiquitous moral obligation.

We have shown the relational nature of positioning—that is, in Enfermada's moral order, one who takes themselves up as responsible for joint lines of action may position the other as not responsible. Or if one takes up the position of being aggrieved in relation to another, then the other is a perpetrator of the injustice. We have shown that what seems obvious from one position, and readily available to any other person, is not necessarily so for the person in the "other" position. The relative nature of positions not only to each other but to moral orders can make the perception of one almost impossible for the other, in the relational position, to grasp.

One's beliefs about the sorts of persons, including oneself, who are engaged in a conversation are central to how one understands what has been said. Exactly what the force of any utterance on a particular occasion is will depend on that understanding.

In demonstrating the shifting nature of positions, depending on the narratives/metaphors/images through which the positioning is being constituted, we have shown how both the social act performed by the uttering of those words and the effect that action has is a function of the narratives employed by each speaker as well as the particular positions that each speaker perceives the other speaker to be taking up.

There are normative expectations at each level. Sano is surprised at Enfermada's protest because according to conventions of the nurse-patient narrative, there is a normative expectation that the poorly both need and accept care. Of course, this narrative also includes the case of the difficult patient. Enfermada for her part is accustomed to being marginalized in men's talk. In hearing him as giving offense she is interpreting him as engaging in normative male behavior. And of course within this narrative men are notoriously unable to recognize the ways in which their taking up of paternalistic positions negates the agency of the women with whom they are interacting.

We have shown the necessity of separating out intended meanings from hearable meanings in the process of developing discursive practices that are not paternalistic or discriminatory *in their effect*. The (personal) political implications of attending to the discursive practices through which one positions oneself, and is positioned, are that one's speech-as-usual with its embedded metaphors, images, forms, etc., can be recognized as inappropriate to personal/political beliefs both of one's own and of others with whom one interacts.

Contradiction, choice, and the possibility of agency

Persons as speakers acquire beliefs about themselves that do not necessarily form a unified coherent whole. They shift from one to another way of thinking about themselves as the discourse shifts and as their positions within varying storylines are taken up. Each of these possible selves can be internally contradictory or contradictory with other possible selves located in different storylines. Like the flux of past events, conceptions people have about themselves are disjointed until and unless they are located in a story. Since many stories can be told, even of the same event, then we each have many possible coherent selves. But to act rationally, those contradictions we are immediately aware of must be remedied, transcended, resolved, or ignored. While it is logically impossible to act from a formally contradictory script—no one could go simultaneously to Boston and New York—most people, most of the time, wittingly or unwittingly accept that their beliefs about themselves and their environment are full of unresolved contradictions that one just lives with. This feature of being human in a Christian universe was much more openly acknowledged in the past, with the concept of "God's mysterious ways." How could a benevolent God create such an unjust world? and so on. The possibility of choice in a situation in which there are contradictory requirements provides people with the possibility of acting agentically.

In making choices between contradictory demands there is:

- a complex weaving together of the positions (and the cultural/social/ political meanings that are attached to those positions) that are available within any number of discourses;

- the emotional meaning attached to each of those positions, which has developed as a result of personal experiences of being located in each position, or of relating to someone in that position;

- the stories through which those categories and emotions are being made sense of;

- and the moral system that links and legitimates the choices that are being made.

Because of the social/grammatical construction of the person as a unitary knowable identity, we tend to assume it is possible to have made a set of consistent choices located within only one discourse. And it is true we do struggle with the diversity of experience to produce a story of ourselves that is unitary and consistent. If we don't, others demand of us that we do. We also discursively produce ourselves as separate from the social world and thus are not aware of the way in which the taking up of one discursive practice or another (not originating in ourselves) shapes the knowing or telling we can do. Thus we experience these selves as if they were our own production. We take on the discursive practices and storylines as if they were our own and make sense of them in terms of our own particular experiences. The sense of continuity that we have in relation to being a particular person is compounded out of continued embodiment and so of spatiotemporal continuity, and shared interpretations of the subject positions and storylines available within them. How to "do" being a particular noncontradictory person within a consistent storyline is learned both through textual and lived narratives.

In feminist narratives the idea of the noncontradictory person inside a consistent storyline can, however, be just what is disrupted. In a study of preschool children and gender (Davies, 1989a), it was observed that children often struggled to interpret feminist narratives in terms of more familiar storylines. One such story was *The Paper Bag Princess* (Munsch, 1980). This is an amusing story about a princess called Elizabeth who goes to incredible lengths to save her prince from a fierce dragon. At the beginning of the story, Princess Elizabeth and Prince Ronald are planning to get married, but then a dragon comes along, burns Elizabeth's castle and clothes, and flies off into the distance carrying Prince Ronald by the seat of his pants. Elizabeth is very angry. She finds a paper bag to wear and follows the dragon. She tricks him into displaying all of his magic powers until he falls asleep from exhaustion. She rushes into the dragon's cave to save Ronald, only to find he does not want to be saved by a princess who is covered in soot and only has an old paper bag to wear. He tells her to go away and to come back when she looks like a real princess. Elizabeth is quite taken aback by this turn of events and says, "Ronald your clothes are really pretty and your hair is very neat. You look like a real prince, but you are a bum." The last page shows her skipping off into the sunset alone and the story ends with the words: "They didn't get married after all."

The apparent intention here is to present a female hero who is not dependent on the prince in shining armor for her happiness, nor for confirmation of who she is. It also casts serious doubt on the concept of the prince who can provide eternal happiness. In this story Elizabeth is not a unitary being. She experiences the multiple and contradictory positionings we each experience in our everyday lives. She is positioned at the beginning as the uncomplicated, happy, and loving princess, living out the romantic narrative of love and happiness ever after. She is then positioned as the dragon's victim, but she rejects this and becomes the active, heroic agent who is in control of the flow of events. She is then positioned as victim by Ronald and again refuses this positioning, skipping off into the sunset, a free agent.

The children's readings of the story do not always tap into these apparent intentions of the author. When the dragon burns Elizabeth's castle and steals Prince Ronald, he also burns her clothes off and makes her very dirty. Some children see her at this point as having magically changed into a bad princess, as if the dragon had cast a spell on her. That badness, because of her nakedness, has negative sexual overtones. Some of the boys are fascinated by her naked and bereft state, but generally it is not Elizabeth who holds their interest so much as the large, powerful, and destructive dragon who has devastated her castle and later goes on to devastate entire landscapes. Other boys perceive Ronald as a hero. They comment on his tennis outfit and the medallion around his neck, which they perceive as a tennis gold medal. One boy even managed to see Ronald as heroic, that is, as a central agent in control of his own fate, even at the point where he was sailing through the air, held by the dragon by the seat of his pants: "I'm glad he held onto his tennis racquet so hard. When you've done that, well, you just have to hold onto your racquet tight and the dragon holds you up."

While many of the children did see Elizabeth as a hero, many others were unable to see her as a genuine hero, and they were equally unable to see her choice to go it alone at the end as legitimate or positive. The dragon, for some, is the powerful male, whose power remains untainted by Elizabeth's trickery. In this hearing of the story, Elizabeth clearly loses her prince, not because she chooses to leave him, but because she is lacking in virtue. Some children believed Elizabeth should have cleaned herself up and then married the prince. The story is heard as if it were a variation of a known storyline in which males are heroes and females are other to those heroes. Elizabeth thus becomes a "normal" (unitary noncontradictory) princess who just got things a bit wrong.

If Elizabeth is read *as princess*, or as one in the role of princess, then the nonfeminist reading can follow almost entirely from an understanding of the *role of princess*. In opening with the sentence "Elizabeth was a beautiful princess," the text inadvertently invites such a reading. The only clue in the first page of the text that this is not the usual kind of princess is a reference to the castle as "hers." According to the nonfeminist reading, the dragon's attack turns Elizabeth into a dirty and bad princess. (Being unitary and noncontradictory, magic is necessary to effect such a change in her.) At the end, when Ronald tells her to clean herself up, he is giving her the information she needs to turn herself back into a "real" princess, in effect breaking the magic spell. In the feminist reading the role of princess is not a dominant interpretive category. In this reading Elizabeth, like a modern woman, is caught up in a shifting set of possibilities now positioned as one with power, now as powerless. Her adventure is one in which she makes her way among the various subject positions available to her and eventually escapes them all.

The children's responses to this story illustrate many of the points we have been making: in particular, the multiple possible interpretations of any speech action, the interactive nature of the move from words spoken (or in this case, words on the page) to the social act that is taken to have occurred, and the intimate relation between perception of the positions in which the various characters find themselves and perception of storylines. It also shows that though the story can in one reading present Elizabeth as acting agentically, in another she can be seen to behave foolishly. The discursive production of oneself or of another as an agent requires the appropriate storyline, and for women caught up in traditional roles, it also requires the availability of discursive practices that allow them to be seen as other than in a fixed role. The many children who heard a nonfeminist story illustrate the resilience of traditional discursive practices through which actions are interpreted as gender-based acts. Thus the move from role to position is both analytically and politically necessary in the study of people in their contemporary everyday worlds.

Conclusion

In moving from the use of role to position as the central organizing concept for analyzing how it is that people do being a person, we have moved to another conception of the relation between people and their conversations. In role-theory the person is always separable from the various roles that they take up; any particular conversation is understood in terms of someone taking on a certain role. The words that are spoken are to some extent dictated by the role and are to be interpreted in these terms. With positioning, the focus is on the way in which the discursive practices constitute the speakers and hearers in certain ways and yet at the same time are resources through which speakers and hearers can attempt to negotiate new positions. A subject position is a possibility in known forms of talk; position is what is created in and through talk as the speakers and hearers take themselves up as persons. This way of thinking explains discontinuities in the production of self with reference to the fact of multiple and contradictory discursive practices and the interpretations of those practices that can be brought into being by speakers and hearers as they engage in conversations.

~

There is in this chapter an omission of the important point made in Chapter 4, "The concept of agency," that relations of power mean that "choice" and "agency" are heavily circumscribed for some groups of people whose actions are not recognized or even recognizable as legitimate by those with power over them. This omission is made good in the next chapter, in which positioning in relation to powerlessness is explored in careful detail.

7 ~ Classroom competencies and marginal positionings

P OWER AND POWERLESSNESS are in one sense transitory—the result of being positioned in one way or another, of being positioned or positioning oneself in terms of one category or another, in terms of one discourse or another, as one who can and should act/speak/write powerfully, or as one who cannot or should not. At the same time, there are structural, generally invisible aspects of current Western discourses that are difficult to escape. In particular, binary logic constitutes the world in hierarchical ways through its privileging of one term or category within the binary and depriving the opposite term of meaning in its own right. The privileged term defines the meaning of the subordinate or dependent term as other to itself: it is thus part of the same through being defined in terms of the same. Being positioned as one who belongs in or is defined in terms of the negative or dependent term can, we argue here, lock people into repeated patterns of powerlessness. Deconstruction is a strategy for displacing the hierarchy, for revealing the dependence of the privileged or ascendant term on its "other" for its own meaning; deconstruction moves to disrupt binary logic and its hierarchical, oppositional constitutive force. In this paper we make a deconstructive move on the binaries adult/child and competent/incompetent student in the context of classroom practice.

In thinking about power and powerlessness in order to write about it here, we draw on our own occasional positioning as powerless. Our strategy will not, however, be to draw on our own conversations where we are positioned as powerless. On the contrary, our analysis will be about the struggle to see from the point of view of those students whom we observe to be powerless in our own and other's classrooms where our own authority as adults and teachers makes it difficult to privilege their perceptions, which often do not easily make sense from where we stand.

Most of the data will be drawn from Robyn's classroom. During the period of her master's candidature, with Bronwyn as supervisor, she videotaped many scenes in her classroom and interviewed her students with a mind to coming to see how classroom order is achieved as a concerted effort between

This chapter was written with Robyn Hunt and was originally published in the *British Journal of Sociology of Education* 15(3) in 1994.

teacher and students. These video-recorded episodes and interviews were the topic of many conversations between us as Robyn struggled to move away from interpreting what she saw and heard when she was interacting with the students in terms of the powerful discourse we have called "teaching-as-usual." From within this discourse the sense she had habitually made was from her category position as teacher, that is, as the one who unquestionably knows what is going on and who has the authority to assert the correctness of that view. The alternative she moved towards was informed by poststructuralist theory. In this shift the binary of teacher and student was made visible, the terms reversed in value and to some extent moved beyond.[1]

In setting out to examine the collaborative constitution of classroom order, Robyn first turned to interactionist and ethnomethodological frameworks to examine her data. These she ultimately found unsatisfying because they provided no way of making sense of so much of what the students said and did. There was a tendency within these frameworks to theorize the individual as unitary (rather than as discursively constituted beings positioned variously within multiple contexts), and an assumption of "reasonableness" of the students—that is, that they would make rational choices to be competent (with a subtext that this would be the competence defined as such by the dominant group). Although these tendencies are not necessarily part of the frameworks, an immersion in poststructuralist theorizing was necessary to make these assumptions visible in Robyn's interpretive strategies when thinking within the discourse of teaching-as-usual.

We will use the concept of marking to develop our analysis. By this we mean that within any binary pair of subject categories (white/black, male/female, teacher/student, heterosexual/homosexual, adult/child, etc.) there is a tendency for the former to be understood as normal and the latter to be the dependent term that takes its meaning in terms of its difference from the former. The first term is the privileged term and is often equated in an unstated way with humanness, normality, and the way anyone would be and could be if they were not "different," that difference being understood as a deviance from the ascendant term. It is a deviance they are not necessarily able to correct, however, since their category membership may specifically preclude the behavior defined as normal for those positioned in the ascendant category.

Within the discourse of teaching-as-usual there is a sense in which competent students are also unmarked in terms of the good/bad student binary. These students, with their teacher, create the context that is recognizable as a classroom. They know "how to behave" and in doing so become members of those social scenes in which the teacher is positioned as authoritative teacher and they are positioned as cooperative students. The achievement of this normal scene is in many ways not visible to any of the participants since it is taken for granted as the way things are in classrooms (Davies, 1983).

Teaching-as-usual can go on without any particular attention being paid to it, because it is obvious: everyone knows what is going on. Those who disrupt this order are "problem students" and are marked as such. The problem is seen to lie in them and is read in terms of their difference from the others. We are particularly interested, here, in making visible those aspects of the dominant discourse, teaching-as-usual, through which their entry into the order of the classroom is made problematic.

These (different) students make the authority relations of the classroom much more visible. That visibility of the coercive, constitutive nature of the context comes about, not necessarily because they struggle against it, but more often, in our observations, in their very struggles to be part of it. An unmarked position is a more comfortable one. It needs no reflection—one simply is a member and is accepted and recognized as such.

In this chapter we will use our readings of a number of episodes in primary school classrooms to examine in detail the various positionings that are available to marked marginal members of classrooms. Five episodes will be drawn from the videotapes Robyn made of her own classroom. The other reading is taken from a videotaped study of a classroom undertaken by Bronwyn and analyzed earlier in Davies and Munro (1987). We use this particular data here both because that earlier paper was a significant one in Robyn's re-reading of her own classroom and also because we find we can say something different about it as a result of the work we have done in writing this chapter and which is integral to the ideas we are exploring here.

In a paper arguing for a different, feminist version of how we might define good science, Donna Haraway suggests there is much to be learned from studies of the world from the perspective of the marked or subjugated, and that any claims to truth are best drawn from such studies of partial and situated experiences. One reason for this claim is that the *positions* from which seeing and knowing are done are more readily visible for marked category positions, whereas those who are habitually positioned in unmarked categories, such as male, white, heterosexual, and the ruling class, often manage to generate an illusion of positionless speaking. Such positionless speaking is, Haraway (1988, pp. 583–54) claims, antithetical to any claim to objective knowledge:

> Many currents in feminism attempt to theorize grounds for trusting especially the vantage points of the subjugated; there is good reason to believe vision is better from below the brilliant space platforms of the powerful. Building on that suspicion, this essay is an argument for situated and embodied knowledges and an argument against various forms of unlocatable, and so irresponsible, knowledge claims. Irresponsible means unable to be called into account. There is a premium on establishing the capacity to see from the peripheries and the depths. But here there also lies a serious danger of romanticising and/or appropriating the vision

of the less powerful while claiming to see from their positions. To see from below is neither easily learned nor unproblematic, even if "we" "naturally" inhabit the great underground terrain of subjugated knowledges. The positionings of the subjugated are not exempt from critical re-examination, decoding, deconstruction, and interpretation; that is, from both semiological and hermeneutic modes of critical inquiry. The standpoints of the subjugated are not "innocent" positions. On the contrary, they are preferred because in principle they are least likely to allow denial of the critical and interpretive core of all knowledge. They are knowledgeable of modes of denial through repression, forgetting, and disappearing acts—ways of being nowhere while claiming to see comprehensively. The subjugated have a decent chance to be on to the god trick and all its dazzling—and, therefore, blinding—illuminations. But *how* to see from below is a problem requiring at least as much skill with bodies and language, with the mediations of vision, as the "highest" technoscientific visualizations.

In this chapter we want to examine classrooms from the positions of the subjugated, the marginal, the marked members of that scene. In doing so we hope to reveal the struggle to see classrooms from the subject positions not only the subject positions made available to children, as opposed to those available to adults, but also from the subject positions[2] made available to and taken up by the less-privileged members of the classrooms we have studied (cf. Davies, 1982). At the same time, we want to reveal the positions from which we speak and from which we have struggled to gain some understanding of the positioning of marginal students. In doing so we want to make more visible what we call teaching-as-usual, which is in some ways akin to Haraway's "god perspective"—so dazzlingly clear that it is blinding. And, finally, we want to look with careful attention to the *how* of learning to see from the subjugated perspective, looking at the minute detail of words and of bodies as students are positioned now one way and now another in the context of classrooms.

An early study of marginal positionings in classrooms is McDermott's beautifully detailed study of children in top and bottom reading groups in a first-grade classroom. In this study he reveals the bodily and concerted way in which success and failure are achieved in this classroom. McDermott locates a number of bodily positionings, which he defines as the "postural-kinesic variant of what people do in taking a position on a particular conversational issue" (1976, p. 95). He borrows this usage from Scheflen (1973), who, in McDermott's words, demonstrates that

a line of action takes work on the part of all participants to that action. A speaker cannot maintain the positioning of a teacher without the help of students, and so on. What is most exciting about Scheflen's notion of positioning is that the people in an interaction, speakers and listeners, teachers and students, take on characteristic [bodily] postures at the same time, in concert with one another. In this way, people are each other's contexts in that they form an environment for each other. (McDermott, 1976, p. 95)

McDermott begins his study by pointing out that we find it difficult to see the orderliness of classroom failure. Children who fail are generally seen as chaotic. He says, "the top group is called orderly ('The children in the top group know how to take turns; they know how to behave'). And the bottom group is most often called chaotic. Most viewers see the bottom group as unruly ('They don't know how to take turns; they don't know how to behave')" (pp. 13–14). But as McDermott points out, the behavior of the children in the bottom group makes a lot of sense if studied in careful detail.

The orderliness of the top group is readily visible. The children take it in turns to read around the circle. They sit "carpentered" to their desks (Figure 1), they form a closed circle that remains unbroken either by themselves or other students for the duration of their lesson. Almost the whole of the videotaped twenty-three minutes of their reading lesson is spent on task: the concerted practice of reading takes place without interruption.

McDermott attends in particular to the bodily positionings of teachers and students in the creation of these contexts. He describes how the teacher and the students organize their bodies in particular ways throughout each reading turn:

Throughout the top group's lesson, the same positioning occurs at the beginning of each turn and lasts until the turn is over. Then the members orient to the turn change by shifting their bodies and attention to the teacher or to the next person to read. And then they shift back into the reading positioning. Thus, the flow of behavior is turn, positioning, juncture, and so on. (pp. 94–95)

In contrast, in the bottom group, the children bid for turns. The bidding process breaks the closed sense of circle and the sense of being on task; it precludes any focus on the story being read; and it breaks up the carpentering to the desk that would signal "we are reading" and we should not be interrupted. McDermott points out that:

This strategy of not calling on the children in the bottom group in a fixed order is used by many teachers as a device for keeping the potentially disorderly children constantly attentive. In fact, this attentional device is even built into the design of reading programs for the problem reader. It has the consequence of giving no one, either teacher or children, any time out from monitoring each other for some idea on what to do next. . . . With each turn to read hanging on the teacher's attention to the details of each child's call for a turn, every interruption of the teacher leaves the group without a procedure for moving into the

Figure 1. "Carpentering to desk" (McDermott, 1976, p. 43)

reading task. . . . [T]he bottom group is interrupted almost 40 times in its thirty minutes at the reading table, as compared to only two interruptions in [the top group's] 23 minutes at the table . . . [A]lmost two-thirds of the interruptions come from the members of the top group entering the table while the bottom group is there or from the teacher dealing with members of the top group as they busy themselves . . . with the individualized work the teacher has organized around the room. (pp. 39–40)

These interruptions from the top group generally occur when the bottom group is not carpentered to the desk as in Figure 1. This may be during bidding (Figure 2), or when the teacher breaks the closed nature of the circle and demonstrates something at the board or asks a student to underline something on the board. When the students are carpentered to the desk there is little invitation to others to move into the group:

[In the top group] [n]o one is looking up, and the members organize their bodies to function much like a fixed territorial unit with a gate of shoulders and elbows marking off the boundaries. [Bidding for a turn], however, allows more opening to visitors, and they often enter and prolong the necessity of the members contextualizing each other in the way that they do in getting a turn. Although the children do not engage outsiders while in this positioning, the teacher sometimes disrupts the children by attending to outsiders, while the bottom group members are struggling to get a turn. For example, she calls the children together and says, "Raise your hands if you can read page 4." The children respond immediately and organize into the [getting-a-turn] positioning. . . . As soon as they are well organized with their hands in the air, the teacher looks out to the rest of the classroom to yell at two members of the top group who are not busy at their work. As

Figure 2. "Getting a turn" (McDermott, 1976, p. 47)

she does this, the children in the bottom group lower their hands and one of them pushes himself out of the group and balances on the back legs of his chair. The teacher then returns and attempts to cajole everyone back to the getting-a-turn positioning by saying, "Nobody can read page 4? Why not?" Side sequences of this type take their toll, and the bottom group spends as much time getting a turn as they do reading. (pp. 48–49)

McDermott's detailed observations make it possible to imagine ourselves in each of the subject positions created in and by these two groups. In one, there is a rhythmic, predictable pleasurable display of oneself as one who knows, who can read; in the other, a display of oneself bidding to read, only to find that others' (more important) agendas come first, that one purposelessly and foolishly has one's arm in the air, displaying oneself as one who wants to read. Shifting out of the circle, out of this display of oneself and the group as people who matter less, tipping your chair skillfully back to display, for a moment, your bodily competence in the world, knowing at the same time that your lowered arm will be recognized as a signal that you have a problem with the text and therefore cannot read.

McDermott's work shows in careful detail the concerted nature of students' work to achieve a reading group. It reveals the common-sense knowledge we have of classrooms, that they must work in a collective way if learning is to take place. At the same time, in the attitude of teaching-as-usual, we think of learning as an individual activity. We assess *individual* performances and take ourselves to be legitimately doing so. Many classroom rules are about ensuring that the work that is done is the assessable product of individual students. The following videotaped episode in Robyn's classroom shows a group of students producing themselves as a group doing reading according to the teacher's definition of how this is to be done. It disrupts the attitude of teaching-as-usual about individual assessable productions. The disruption became visible because of the teacher's adoption of position other than teacher: she was also viewing the class in a detailed way as one who wants to understand how she and they produce particular kinds of classroom order. What follows is Robyn's reading of the students' production of the reading circle as she came to see it through viewing and reviewing the video recording of it.

Achieving a reading circle

A group of eight students is seated in a circle on the floor with their teacher. She asks for a volunteer to commence reading. Jamie starts, the other students being required to follow in their books and to wait for their turn to read. Turns are allocated on a volunteer basis but everyone eventually has to read. They understand "everyone will have a turn." The group proceeds to read, each in turn until Leigh is the only person not to have "volunteered":

> *Robyn:* Leigh, would you like to read? [*long pause*] It's your turn. [*Leigh raises his book and leans over towards Jamie. Jamie "shuffles" over towards Leigh. Jamie proceeds to read by leaning close to Leigh and saying each word softly near his ear in such a way that his activity is not easy to see or hear. Leigh "reads" by repeating each word one-at-a-time as Jamie speaks them. Jamie holds the reader in front of his face. None of the students comment on this, verbally or nonverbally. All seem to accept "Leigh is reading." He completes his turn.*]

The students in this episode complied with Robyn's definition of this situation: "This is an oral reading lesson in which you will each read." They remained seated and attended to their books during the entire episode. Confident readers volunteered eagerly but all students accepted that they would have a turn and would "read." Leigh, although reluctant, demonstrated his commitment to school and a willingness to work within Robyn's definition of the situation, though he knew the task he was required to perform in her definition of it was beyond him. He accepted the condition "I must read." With some specific assistance from Jamie and with whole-group cooperation, he found a way to comply with the condition that everyone must read that required disrupting the teaching-as-usual assumption that "reading" is an individual rather than a group task, at the same time leaving this assumption intact for the teacher by keeping their action invisible. These eight students, and Jamie in particular, collaborated to enable Leigh to position himself as one who is willing and able to participate in the teacher's agenda. They

Figure 3. Jamie shuffles towards Leigh

knew, unlike the teacher, until that point, that such a positioning must be a group rather than an individual production.

Later, Robyn talked to Leigh and Jamie about Leigh's reading:

1. *Robyn:* I wanted to ask you two about . . . do you like reading, Leigh?
2. *Leigh:* Yes. [*quietly*]
3. *Robyn:* You don't mind when it's your turn to read? [*pause*] I sort of noticed a couple of times that you seemed a little nervous and I notice how Jamie was helping you. [*pause*] Do you realize how he helps you when it's reading time? [*to Jamie*] What do you do?
4. *Jamie:* I help him say what the words are.
5. *Robyn:* Yeah. [*to Leigh*] How does that make you feel?
6. *Leigh:* I don't know.
7. *Robyn:* Do you like it when Jamie helps you read?
8. *Leigh:* [*Nods.*]
9. *Robyn:* Yeah, yeah it's nice when you've got someone to. [*to Jamie*] How did you decide that you ought to help Leigh?
10. *Jamie:* I don't know. [*pause*] I just knew he didn't know what the words were so I helped him.
11. *Robyn:* And how do you know that?
12. *Jamie:* He couldn't say them.

This was an interesting conversation, presumably for all the participants. The teacher had stepped out of her teaching-as-usual perspective to ask the students how they constructed a scene that they knew could be called from that more usual perspective "cheating." The teacher had to position herself as one not making such judgments—that is, for the moment, interacting with them as a researcher who wanted to privilege their knowledges rather than her own. They had to cautiously assess the position she was speaking from to know the import of her questions and therefore how to answer them. The correct answer to the questions in 1 and 3 might have been "I can't read" and Leigh responds either softly or with silence throughout. When the teacher positions Jamie as helper (3), rather than, say, as one who has collaborated in an episode of cheating, Jamie picks up and uses this word (4, 10) to position himself as someone who behaved properly in response to what seemed obvious, that Leigh could not do what was required in a reading lesson as it is collectively defined in this context unless someone told him the words.[3]

The achievement of coherent workable collectives can thus be read as something the students negotiated, sometimes at the risk of being defined as behaving against the teacher's agenda in which assessable individual work was central to the work she took herself to be doing as a teacher. However, it appears that if the students defined a particular class member as unable or unwilling to work to achieve such concerted activity, as in the following episode, they sometimes excluded that student from the collectives they were creating. Coherently carrying out the teacher's agenda (for example, doing cooperative group work) could not be done with someone in the group who did not know the detailed work required to sustain group work. Jason was well known for being a disruptive student. Robyn had been working with him to teach him some of the behaviors that would achieve for him the identity "cooperative student," an identity he appeared to covet. But the other students appeared to be more attentive to the difficulty of achieving concerted group activity with Jason present than they were of the individual program being developed for Jason and of Robyn's unstated requirement that they would give him opportunities to practice his new repertoire, to be one of them, rather than one recognized and known as disruptive. In the following videotaped episode Robyn finds herself, from her teaching-as-usual perspective, assuming that her instruction to form groups would be followed in relation to her specific agenda of including Jason and not simply their (and her) agenda of achieving workable groups. In this episode it is possible to see the competent (unmarked) students at risk of becoming marked, positioned as incompetent students who do not know how to behave and so have to be told what to do. The risk they face, in this reading, is of shifting from a powerful positioning to a powerless one.

Negotiating entry

The class was involved in an oral language activity. For this task the students were asked to divide themselves into four groups. The site of each group was designated by the teacher, the particular membership of each group determined by the students. After two minutes groups were formed involving all the children except Jason, who was now sitting on the outside and just to the right of one of the small-group circles.

1. *Robyn:* Is there a problem there, Jason?
2. *Jason:* I haven't got a circle.
3. *Robyn:* Yes, you do. Join one of them please. [*Jason remains seated on the floor and "caterpillars" himself towards the circle on his right by stretching out his legs and sliding his body towards his feet. The class waits while the caterpillar movements put Jason just on the outside of the circle he was approaching. Jason stops. No one in the circle attempts to move to create a space for Jason in the circle. Jason looks towards Robyn. Craig and John remain seated with their backs to Jason. They turn their heads to look towards the teacher. The class and the teacher wait.*]
4. *Robyn:* Boys, I want this resolved, please. We have a lesson to get on with. [*Jason continues to look towards the teacher. No one in the circle moves.*] Jason is a member of this class and I expect that he'll be allowed to do the things I ask him to do. [*The class and the teacher wait. Craig and John look at each other. Jason remains on the outside of the circle. Craig shuffles slowly away from John, creating a small space within the circle. The class and the teacher wait while one more half caterpillar movement places Jason's body half in the circle. He stops and looks towards the teacher.*] In your groups I'd like you to . . .

Although the detailed description of this video already implies much of our reading of it, we will pursue further the detail of what we can see in looking at it this way. Jason is asked to account for his failure to be part of the concerted activity of forming a series of groups such that each person is a member of a group (1). His account that he hasn't got a circle is not accepted as valid and he is told to make himself into a member of a group (3). He moves towards a group, but the group does not act in concert with him, making a space for him to enter. The entire class, including Jason, then engages in the concerted activity of waiting to see what the teacher will say (3). Craig and John, by not acting in concert with Jason, are opposing what the teacher wants at that moment, and in so doing are maintaining the possibility of their positioning as powerful students who can do what she wants, that is, form a group that can engage in the concerted effort necessary for successful group activity. Their positioning of themselves is not accepted as a competent positioning. They must, in order to remain competent, read the necessity in Robyn's agenda of having Jason included as one of the collective. Moreover, they must *choose* to include him. Robyn insists that Jason is a member of the class (4) and thus has the right of entry to a class group. Jason moves towards the group, the group opens up to let him in as a partial member, and the teacher accepts this as meeting her requirements, signaling this by commencing instructions for the activity of the groups: "In your groups I'd like you to . . ."(4).

Unlike Leigh in the previous episode, Jason is not positioned by the other students as one who can pass himself off as a successful class member in concerted activity with the rest of the group.

Students like Jason create a dilemma not just for the teacher but also for the other students. For our purposes here, they make visible the authority of the teacher in the (willing) creation by the students of the concerted activity of making a classroom. They also make it possible to see the ways in which students are reliant on each other for the successful production of themselves as competent individuals in the classroom, since the reading of them as competent individuals relies heavily on their ability to enter and be part of concerted group activity.

It is interesting to compare the refusal of entry here with Corsaro's observations of preschool children gaining entry to each other's group play (1979). In his observation, those who were most successful in gaining entry tended to stand outside the group for a period of time watching the game being played. Following this period of observation, successful entry was not usually accomplished by a request to enter, nor a suggestion of a different kind of activity. Rather, it was accomplished by an inclusion of self into the ongoing flow of the game. The successful would-be entrant behaved as if s/he already belonged to the group and demonstrated this belonging by uttering lines that could be interpreted as part of the play in progress.

But what if one cannot be recognized, despite knowledge of such strategies, as one who can utter such lines? In Bronwyn's study of preschool children, for example, the difficulty of girls gaining access to the dominant group of boys' activity as one of them, rather than as female other to their heroic games, was often evident. Joanne, an extremely accomplished player, could remember only once when the boys allowed her to be the hero in their game of Voltron. They demanded that she be the princess who could be attacked and saved. That was probably much more satisfying to them, since they constantly had the problem of finding suitable victims for their heroic games, and their accomplishment of themselves as heroic within the cultural storylines available to them did not include playing with a powerful female other who could dictate their moves. So Joanne refused to play with them on those terms and waited around the edges, watching, hoping that her friend Tony would leave the group and come and play with her. One way she accomplished this was to get an exciting line of action going with other marginal children who became her victims and who could be abandoned once Tony had joined her (Davies, 1989a).

But in the classroom such innovations are more difficult. The line of action is dictated by the teacher. The choice is limited to what is legitimate within the discourse of teaching-as-usual. Students might be invited to form groups—they can say who is in and who is out as long as there are no people who have been made outsiders by everyone. The game is much more complex than musical chairs. It is not enough to find one's own place, to be in the game. The outsiders who are not-our-group (and who thus in part define our group) must also be attended to. This struggle around boundaries, of what makes a group, of what it means to be asked to form one's own group, was in part what the struggle around Jason's membership can be seen to be about. But it was also about Jason's history within the classroom as it was seen by the participants, which was such that he could not be seen as one who was an acceptable member, no matter what new strategies he might currently be working on to acquire the means of signaling "I am an acceptable member."

Competent membership

As Walkerdine and Lucey (1989) point out, many of the strategies that are brought by competent students to the school and the classroom are a taken-for-granted part of the interactional practices they have learned in interacting with their mothers. What teachers and other competent students read as "I belong" and "I am a successful participant in this scene" may well have little to do with individual "choice," though choice is the dominant paradigm through which an individual's actions are interpreted. Jason was learning as a set of consciously acquired strategies from Robyn how to signal belonging, since both she and he had no doubt that he wanted to belong. Other students, such as Jody in the following episode, were more difficult to read as wanting to belong. Much of her presentation of self appeared to run so far counter to what a competent student would do that it defied imagination within the teaching-as-usual discourse to think of her as other than marginal by choice, deliberately and irrationally signaling her refusal of the category position competent student.

The following episode began with Robyn interviewing Jody about a written task she had asked her to complete. At the time, she was gathering data with the students on the concept of "competence" and would talk with them as opportunities arose during lessons. While she tried to focus on the purpose of the conversation with Jody she was continually distracted by Jody's very purple hair. How could wearing purple hair to school possibly be compatible with an interest in or knowledge of competent school behaviors?

1. *Robyn:* Do you know what I really wanted to ask you about [*pause*] was your hair. How come it's purple?

2. *Jody:* 'Cause I was goin' out.

3. *Robyn:* Uh huh. Was that your idea or mum's?

4. *Jody:* Mum's.

5. *Robyn:* Do the kids tease you about that?

6. *Jody:* Yeah.

7. *Robyn:* How do you feel when they tease you?

8. *Jody:* Not very good.

9. *Robyn:* Uh huh. They can be a bit cruel sometimes, can't they. What sort of things do you do when they start to tease you?

10. *Jody:* Just ignore 'em and go away.

11. *Robyn:* Is that what mum told you to do?

12. *Jody:* No, she never told me nothink.

It was the conversations with Jody more than any other that led Robyn to be able to see the way her expectations were embedded in the discourse of teaching-as-usual and to an intense search for a different way of making sense of what she saw. The question "How come it's purple?" was asked because it appeared to Robyn to be contradictory with any serious or sincere effort to be an acceptable student (1). From Jody's point of view it was apparently simple—she was goin' out and Mum had thought purple hair appropriate (4). And Mum, apparently, had not seen the purple hair as incompatible with what was required of Jody at school. Robyn's questioning also assumed that if other kids tease you for having purple hair, any rational person, knowing this, would not choose to come to school with purple hair (5–9). And whereas Robyn imagined work on the part of the mother to hand Jody the strategies for dealing with the (obvious) incongruity between purple hair and the achievement of oneself as student, Jody's mum had told her "nothink" (11, 12). What had seemed obvious was no longer necessarily so. If the obviousness of Jody's perception is accepted, she can no longer be read as irrational, insincere, or delinquent. She was simply at school with purple hair because she was goin' out. Her positioning as marginal was no longer inevitable in Robyn's viewing of it, since her assumption of the correctness and dominance of her own interpretive strategies, and thus of teaching-as-usual, had been successfully disrupted.

Another feature of Jody's behavior that marked her as other to the good students was her handwriting. It was below the standard that Robyn had defined as the acceptable level for that grade. Such "standards" are part and parcel of the usually unquestioned knowledges that make teachers recognizable as teachers. Their task is to insist that students come up with the appropriate level. It is assumed that "trying harder" will produce the right results, that is, that genuine commitment to being a good student will be revealed by having tried hard enough. Jody had thus often been asked to do her work again in an appropriate way. In the following videotaped episode Jody brought to Robyn's desk work completed for assessment in exceptionally good writing that signaled at last that she had tried hard enough.

1. *Robyn:* Wow, Jody that's the best writing I've ever seen from you. You've been trying hard. [*Robyn looks approvingly at the bookwork, reaches into the drawer and finds a sticker and puts it on Jody's work.*]
2. *Jody:* Yeah.
3. *Robyn:* Well, I'm impressed. That's terrific. [*Robyn puts another sticker on Jody. Long pause. Robyn continues to look approvingly at Jody's work. Jody looks at the sticker in her book and then at the sticker on her chest.*]
4. *Jody:* I never done that. [*points to her book*]
5. *Robyn:* What do you mean?
6. *Jody:* Nikki done it for me. [*screws up her nose and smiles*]

In our reading of this episode, Jody, like Leigh earlier, had found a way to produce for Robyn what she wanted, even though this was outside the range of competencies that Jody herself possessed. The trouble in the classroom and the trouble for Jody in continually having to do the work over had been averted. Nikki had produced for Jody what was required in this classroom. When Robyn applauds the work in the book (1), Jody assents (2). Robyn marks the book with her approval. Jody does not protest. She has produced good work and Robyn is pleased. Then Robyn marks Jody's body with a stamp of approval and Jody presumably finds herself with a problem. She has a moral dilemma. While the work is good, Jody is not the author of it. That her intention was not to deceive but to give Robyn what was required in this classroom is revealed by her highly risky claim "I never done that" (4). Unlike Leigh, she does not use silence to protect her from the possible accusation of cheating, and in response to Robyn's stunned question (5) she explains that Nikki is the author of the work. This is a profound moment in terms of positioning. Jody has achieved the good work required in this classroom. She has established her moral integrity in not accepting the illusion that it was her hand that created the work—the sticker on her chest is not there legitimately. She then manages with her smile and her screwed-up nose to position herself as one who is not confronting the teacher or being naughty or smart, but simply as one who is telling the truth, awkward as that truth might be. Again, what had once seemed obvious to Robyn was totally disrupted. There was an obviousness about the difference between the concerted production of a classroom and individual work. That obviousness could no longer hold. The class knew that it was not Jody's work, but they were not going to say so. Collectively, they produced a trouble-free classroom and made Jody one of them. They teased her about her hair probably for much the same reasons, as part of a strategy for letting her know that she was not successfully able to achieve herself as having legitimate access to an unmarked category position if she dyed her hair purple.

Had Robyn responded to Jody's "confession" by reprimanding her for dishonest conduct she would then be positioned as a "dishonest person" in a storyline based on the teaching-as-usual discourse. From the alternative perspective Robyn was beginning to develop through such close study of the videotaped interactions and the interviews that privileged the children's perceptions, Jody's action was readable as highly moral. She positioned herself as one who would not falsely claim praise for herself, while still struggling to produce herself as the sort of person she was required to be in the classroom context, that is, as one who makes the classroom visible and workable as a classroom. She is powerless as child to Robyn's adult—she must strive to be competent in Robyn's terms. She is powerless to produce the work a good student would produce with her own hand. At the same time, she is powerful in her capacity to position herself as this moral person who has made an investment of herself in a moral discourse from which she chooses to speak. She is also powerful in her capacity to signal that she sees the dilemma and is not confronting Robyn's authority. For such a positioning to be possible, it was necessary not only that Robyn read it as such but probably also that Jody be aware that Robyn was capable of doing so. It is this reading of Robyn's capability that makes the shift here, which allows Jody to be read as competent classroom member and Robyn as one who is constituted, through Jody's reading, as competent teacher.

We want to move, finally, to an episode in another classroom. This episode was recorded when the teacher invited Bronwyn to videotape her classroom rather than the classrooms she was currently working on in the school. The invitation was issued as a challenge to come and see what "real" classrooms were like. At the time this episode was recorded, the teacher had, in consultation with the school counselor, decided to use behavior management strategies with Lenny, a student who was well known for his noncooperation in classroom scenes and with whom her existing strategies had not worked. The teacher had invited the other students to ignore Lenny until he had achieved the detailed behavior that she judged as constituting good student behavior. Only good behavior would warrant attention from her. The student was thus working without any of the detailed cues in which students create contexts for each other that are recognizably one kind of context or another. What we want to show in our reading of Lenny's interaction in this classroom, drawing on the insights from the previously analyzed episodes, is that Lenny's behavior also makes sense. It is not as chaotic as it first appears.

Being positioned as not visible within and by the collective

Lenny is seated at a table with several other students. John is next to him and Michael across from him. All three are Aboriginal. They are thus in a further marked category, Aboriginal as opposed to white. Most of the other children in the class are white. Each student in the classroom is expected to be getting on with his or her own work as the teacher moves from one individual to another. Lenny has an exercise book in front of him, but he does not appear to have been given individual work to get on with. He attempts a number of times to signal that he is a competent student. He carpenters himself to the desk; he says he wants some work. He uses phrases out of the children's popular American television program *Welcome Back Kotter* to signal that he reads this as a classroom and that he is recognizably the kind of student that he sees on this program. However, none of these signals are read by the teacher as achieving a successful positioning as competent student and therefore none of them warrant a response. In each case Lenny's signaling "I am a student" lapses and he looks for other ways of positioning himself as one who has access to a recognizable positioning in this context:

1. *Lenny:* [*Lenny is seated as in Figure 4 with his legs casually up on the desk, leaning back in his chair. He calls out loudly.*] Hey miss, hey Mr. Kotter, Mr. Kotter! [*John reaches across in front of Lenny for some Cuisenaire rods. Lenny repositions himself slightly and looks in the direction of the teacher. No eye contact is achieved. The teacher does not acknowledge Lenny.*] Fuck. Mr. Bloody Kotter, ya ( ) [*Lenny shifts his legs down and sits in a "good pupil" position carpentered to the desk as in Figure 5.*] Hey man, I want some work over here! [*Lenny looks up in the teacher's direction. She does not look in his direction.*] Hey [*bangs elbow on desk*] Mr. Kotter [*annoyed tone of voice*]. [*He leans back in the chair and puts his legs up on the desk. The teacher walks past while he is in the middle of this action, touches him lightly on the head as she passes and moves on to attend to Jenny.*] I want some work down here. [*He waves his pencil and bangs his paper on the desk.*]

2. *Teacher:* When you sit quietly I'll come and see you. [*She moves back past him, tapping him lightly on the leg.*] Sit round so that I can ( ). When you sit nicely I'll come back and see you. [*Teacher attends to other students. Lenny persuades John to play with him and the teacher directs John back to his work. Lenny attempts and fails to draw John back into his game. He then sits up and carpenters himself to the desk.*] Is Lenny behaving himself so I can come and have a look at his work? [*Teacher begins to move towards Lenny. He raises his book and waves it in the air before dropping it back on to the desk.*]

3. *John:* No. Look what he's doing [*points to Lenny's book and desk*].

4. *Teacher:* [*To John*] You just get on with your work. [*She is still on her way towards Lenny. He sits up straight, carpentered to the desk. Two girls approach the teacher and she stops to look at their work.*]

5. *Lenny:* [*softly*] Move it ladies, move it. [*The teacher continues to talk to the girls. Lenny swears.*]

6. *Teacher:* I think we're going to ignore Lenny for talking until he behaves himself. [*Lenny grabs at the book the teacher is showing one of the girls and she shakes it loose. Lenny softly calls out "Mr. Kotter" and then grabs Michael's ruler. Michael demands it back and Lenny whaps it on the desk. The teacher comes round and sits down beside Lenny. As she moves into the sitting position he puts his foot on the rung of the chair she is going to sit on, sliding his knees forward so the space under the desk is blocked. As the teacher pulls the chair out and sits down she bumps Lenny's legs against the table.*]

7. *Lenny:* Ouch! [*John leans across him for more rods.*]

8. *Teacher:* ( ) If you had your legs under the table I wouldn't have to tread on your feet. Right, how are we going? [*She looks at Lenny's book. Lenny swings around away from her and stands up. She grabs him by his jumper, two hands on his waist stopping him from leaving.*]

9. *Lenny:* Hey man! [*She pulls him back into his seat.*] I'm going somewhere. [*She pulls Lenny's chair closer to her and parallel to the desk.*]

10. *Michael:* [*Reaches across and hits Lenny with a rule*] You stay there!

11. *Teacher:* [*Reprimands and waves finger at Michael*] Ah uh ah! [*Lenny leaps up and threatens Michael. The teacher pulls him back and begins a lesson with the Cuisenaire rods. He doesn't know the value of the rod the teacher shows him and John tells him which one it is.*] Right. Can you write 5? [*Lenny leans over his book. The teacher passes John a rod and then turns around to attend to the girls who have come to stand behind her. While she attends to them Lenny gets up and continues his fight with*

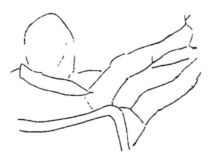

Figure 4. Lenny's feet on desk

Michael. His lesson is over. During the next few minutes Lenny's behavior escalates into picking up chairs and desks, swearing most colorfully at John, and then climbing out the window and swinging from the beams outside. The other students all rush to watch him out the window and one of them closes the window so he cannot get back in and has to drop a considerable distance to the ground below.][4]

Lenny's "cool" posture (1) is not competent student behavior as it is understood in this classroom. His first positioning of himself, then, is not in terms of the classroom order as it is defined here, but as it is defined in the *Kotter* series in which the students, known as sweathogs, are supercool, black and ethnically "different," humorous, and much liked by their teacher. His bid for attention from the teacher is framed as if she were Mr. Kotter and thus as if she would accept his cool style as an acceptable, if unusual, way of being a student. He looks in her direction, but no contact is made, no calibration of his action and her action is made possible. Lenny swears at the teacher, who is not behaving as Mr. Kotter does, "Fuck. Mr. Bloody Kotter." She has not entered into the storyline he has initiated. He moves into the posture McDermott calls being carpentered to the desk and which signals attending to one's work. He continues to use sweathog speaking style but this time is more explicit about the fact that he has no work and wants some. If getting on with individual work is what the students are all supposed to be doing, Lenny cannot be a student as that is currently defined unless he has some work that he can do. Again, he looks at her and again there is no contact, no possibility of calibration. His annoyance is visible in his voice as he bangs on the desk and calls out to her. She walks behind him, touching him, signaling she is aware of his presence but that no interaction is to take

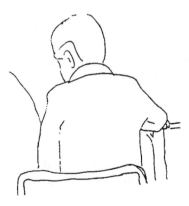

Figure 5. Lenny carpentered to desk

place. He resumes his cool position with feet on the desk. Two positionings have now failed, one as a sweathog, the other as a good student carpentered to the desk and asking for work. His swearing was presumably more visible to the teacher than his posture and his request for work. (It has been shown elsewhere how difficult teachers find it to hear swearing as anything other than a confrontation even when this is not confrontative within the student's home dialect [Werthman, 1971].) But even with his feet back on the desk, he still asks for work. He thus indicates that the posture is not, in his understanding of what it means to be a student, incompatible with work.

The teacher finally addresses him (2), telling him that *speaking at all* is incompatible with being a student who might get attention. In other words, if he suffered from the illusion that it was possible for him to initiate action or to define the kind of action that might be, he can rid himself of that illusion. Silence is all that will gain him attention. He is quiet, so she adds a further instruction. He must sit "nicely," presumably meaning carpentered to the desk as if he were working. As the teacher then goes on to engage with other students (who are free to walk around the classroom and still get attention), Lenny gets a different line of action going with John. But John is removed from him as someone he can interact with and Lenny is again returned to the solitary problem of positioning himself as *someone* in this classroom. He tries to engage John and fails and then sits carpentered to the desk (2).

The teacher addresses the class, asking whether Lenny is "behaving" himself. John makes the mistake of answering and is told to get on with his work. John's answer is similar to the group treatment of Jason. Lenny is outside, marginal, and John is not willing or perhaps able to find ways to bring Lenny in as a member. So far, in fact, Lenny has dangerously drawn him out, made him at risk of being a marginal member. By his "no" John realigns himself with those who know what good student behavior is, though he does not get it exactly right as he apparently does not realize that silence is what is required at this point. Lenny remains in his "nice" sitting position and the teacher, following her question, is clearly heading towards him. But other students are allowed to take precedence, just as the top readers in McDermott's study were able to routinely interrupt the bottom reading group. Lenny's opportunity to get some work to start with is interrupted before it happens. Lenny protests (5) and is again positioned as one who cannot be attended to (6).

The teacher finally arrives to work with Lenny. Until now she has interacted with students by leaning over their work or by standing and talking to them. She goes to sit down beside Lenny and he moves to block her. She bangs his leg against the table and when he expresses pain she tells him that he was hurt because he was sitting incorrectly. He attempts to escape and she forces him into the chair (6). All of Lenny's cool disappears when the teacher moves into this close teaching position. We can only guess at why.

Maybe the fact that he won't be able to perform, despite his earlier bravado, will now be revealed and he doesn't want that. Perhaps he objects to her moving so close, when others are able to keep more of a distance. Perhaps his experiences with teachers at close range are all so negative that he literally panics at the close proximity of one of these people who, in all his years of schooling, appear to have taught him nothing of the content of school learning and much about the experience of powerlessness. But she pulls him back to a sitting position.

Michael at this point intervenes, telling him in a threatening way to stay in his seat (10). Michael seems less concerned with doing the teacher's work for her than in instructing Lenny to engage in competent student behavior. He is, after all, always potentially aligned with Lenny in a joint membership of the marked category Aboriginal. His initiative is rejected by the teacher. She positions him as one who has stepped out of line and begins work with Lenny. Lenny doesn't know the answer and so John supplies it (another chance for John to position himself as good student, which is this time accepted [11]). Lenny is instructed to write John's answer in his book and at this moment two girls are allowed to interrupt the lesson with Lenny. He uses this distraction to escape and to rush around and take up his interaction with Michael. He appears to recognize at this point that two can play at the teacher's game. If she is going to ignore him, he can get away with anything and his imagination carries him to some quite dramatic lengths. He becomes central and visible in everyone's eyes instead of invisible, and while not a competent student or member of the class, he is decidedly recognizably someone.

The teacher's teaching-as-usual attitude took no account of and did not therefore use the considerable knowledges of students to engage in concerted activity. The help she might have gained from Michael and John is refused. Lenny is positioned as an outsider who must somehow find the right pattern of behavior so that he can be positioned as in. But being in, while extraordinarily difficult to achieve, is hardly worth it. He gets literally only a few seconds of "teaching" and is instantly abandoned in favor of others. The minute, detailed readings that students must do to find out what appropriate behavior is in any situation in order to concertedly create that situation are not recognized. Teaching-as-usual defines the children as simply obedient or disobedient to the teacher's instructions, which she takes to be obvious and easily followed by anyone who wishes or intends to be positioned as a competent student. The difficulty of positioning oneself as a student with no work to do, with no legitimate words to speak, and apparently with no basic skills is apparently not visible.

We do not wish to suggest that Lenny's actions throughout this episode were conscious calculated ones. In analyzing the stories of opera Clément (1988, p. 165) talks of the way the lived history of being in the world functions in the present in a nonlinear fashion, making things relevant that need not rationally be so but are so nonetheless:

> [T]he events resemble and thwart one another, the second both annulling and repeating the first. To see these correlations, one must stop listening to the narrative in chronological order and leap backwards, anachronistically . . . [like] the unconscious[, which] could not care less about time passing and the order of events, and it never stops recalling events in the past that it places in the present. That can be called a lapse or an abortive action; more generally it is part of an essential process that Freud calls delayed reaction, a reaction after the fact, but also always a reaction in advance, because the traces that are permanently inscribed make you act and make choices that are somehow knowable in advance. There too, bundles of relations are operating, which are opposite and supplemental to the life you lead—that you believe you "lead" but that, in fact, leads you.

Conclusion

In the discourse of teaching-as-usual both students and teachers are caught up in the subject positions made possible and, in some cases, inevitable, by that discourse. No one has unequivocal and permanent power here, though the marked positions of student, and in particular bad/incompetent student, make it extraordinarily difficult to position oneself as powerful and extremely unlikely that one will be positioned by others as having power, or able to act in powerful or agentic ways. In many cases they do not even find it possible to speak at all or in ways that can be heard as legitimate. This does not mean that a student like Lenny cannot occasionally capture the entire scene, though almost inevitably to his own eventual detriment, since from the position of teacher in the teaching-as-usual discourse his behavior cannot be read as legitimate protest. Lenny would need skills quite other than those he has in order to draw others with him in creating any serious questioning of the dominant discourses that position him as outside schooling-as-usual. As it is, it is a solitary and lonely protest in which both teacher and students shut him out. Ironically, if he did have such skills, the press of the schooling context and its dominant discourses would probably be such that he would use those skills to position himself as competent student and not as one who disrupts.

So how did Robyn manage to disrupt the certainty and power of her unmarked position?

She did so primarily by looking at the detailed ways in which the students produced the contexts in which teaching-as-usual could proceed, despite its almost impossible demands that the students both produce an orderly collective and within that collective produce themselves as individual competent students in the teacher's terms and apparently independently of the collective. Fundamental to this production of the competent, independent student are a set of liberal humanist assumptions about the nature of persons: that they are predominantly rational beings whose rationality is signaled by the fact that they would choose to be recognized as competent within the terms of the dominant discourses; that they are unitary noncontradictory beings who can use reason to choose between being powerful and competent or powerless and incompetent; that virtue and effort and competence are closely related elements of any person's being; and that lack of virtue or competence signals insufficient effort rather than the fact of being positioned inside a discursive structure that marks the one so positioned as marginal and incompetent or not making the right sort of effort. It is this shift to the recognition of discursive structures, and the binaries within them, that shapes the interpretive possibilities we see and the positions we take up, that is central to the deconstruction of the unmarked position of the teacher-as-one-who-knows.

One of the things we have not brought into the discussion is our own experiences of being positioned as powerless and the key part they played in allowing us to imagine moving into the positions of those who were other to us and to disrupt their otherness and difference. During the time Robyn was undertaking this study, she had her teaching assessed for the purposes of promotion. The inspector was unable to see her involvement in this project and her choice to manage her classroom differently as legitimate because it fell outside what he had already defined as the criteria for a good classroom. Even though Robyn's classroom was by then being used as a model for teachers with problem students to see how working constructively with those students might be done, she was not able to be seen as correct within the terms of the dominant discourse through which she was being defined as nonpromotable. The anger and powerlessness that she experienced at the unreasonableness of those making this judgment, and her positioning in her conversations with Bronwyn as having a valid position from which to be angry, were critical in enabling her to see how her own students might feel when she positioned them in the same way—that is, as ones who have no way of being heard outside the discursive categories dictated by the dominant classroom discourse. With this in mind, it gradually became self-evident that it was the students who were creating order in her classroom, despite her sometimes contradictory and impossible demands. At the same time, with the aid of poststructuralist discourse she could disrupt the assumption that her own position and the positions of the competent students were the only "normal" and reasonable ones available and instead begin to see from the multiple possible positions available in the classroom. Just as she would have liked the inspector to see her innovations as legitimate, so she assumed that difference was not deviance or confrontation but something interesting to be listened to. The "problem" students were no longer "other" in the usual sense of deviating from an ascendant norm, but other in a range of multiple possibilities, each of which made sense from the positions they were standing in and the discourses that were available to them for meaning-making.

~

The explorations of poststructuralist theory and of the ways in which it can be used and extended both to make sense of everyday life and to make sense of questions of gender and of power and powerlessness, which have been unfolding throughout this book, were interrupted in a rather startling way by a published attack on my work (Jones, 1997), claiming that my work misleads those who read it into mistaken and undesirable bouts of humanism. The readers were enjoined to avoid reading my work and instead to read Butler. I made a detailed reply to the attack, part of which I include in the next chapter. I have not included the detailed textual analysis of the paper by Jones, as that is interesting only after reading her text. What I do include is the revisiting of concepts she calls "humanist" and the discussion as to whether they can and should be regarded as usable concepts within poststructuralist writing.

Notes

1. The binary supervisor/student in which the supervisor has superior knowledge is one Bronwyn strove constantly to disrupt, recognizing nevertheless that she had had more practice in reading the details of classrooms from multiple perspectives and that she had an obligation to make her insights available to Robyn whenever they seemed useful in relation to the particular questions Robyn was asking of her data. When we wrote this paper, Bronwyn regarded it as Robyn's paper, a paper about her classroom and her achievement of a different reading of it. Robyn regarded it as really Bronwyn's paper because she had taken the major responsibility for writing it. We agreed in the end that we were both deeply satisfied with what we had jointly produced and that ownership was irrelevant.

2. We use two similar terms in this paper, subject position and category position. The former we take to be the subjectively experienced positioning of a category made available in the discursive practices through which one is constituted. The latter we use when specifically referring to the linguistic usage rather than the subjective experience of it.

3. The work that Jamie was doing to assist Leigh in the positioning of himself as one who takes a reading turn is not incompatible with some reading schemes that suggest the strategy of hearing and seeing the word at the same time and then saying it.

4. Shortly afterwards, Bronwyn left the room, worried that her presence might be contributing to the problem. Lenny was clearly aware of the camera, glancing in the direction of the camera and giggling when he produced some of his more extreme epithets. That the situation was not somehow created because Bronwyn was there was evidenced by the fact that neither teacher nor students treated this event with any surprise. No one even flinched when Lenny lurched around the classroom with a chair held aloft over his head. As well, when Bronwyn met her own children (then primary school–age) that afternoon, still amazed at what she had seen and wanting to talk about it, they responded on hearing her description with "oh we know who that is." He had been in their classrooms and his identity was instantly recognizable from the events she described. Evidently it was not the individual teacher who was causing Lenny to behave in the way he did but the patterns and assumptions of teaching-as-usual that give Lenny no way of being positioned as a competent student.

8 ~ The subject of poststructuralism

IN HER ATTACK ON MY WORK, Alison Jones (1997) makes an exposition of the problems her students face in acquiring poststructuralist discourse that I am intrigued by, since I see my own students engaging in similar struggles. I am also intrigued by her finding in my writing an (unwitting) incitement of her students to unwanted bouts of confused humanism. Active verbs, such as "positioning" and "choice," and terms such as "agency" incorrectly invoke, according to Jones, a "prediscursive" humanist subject. The subject as it is understood in poststructuralism, in contrast, can only engage in *apparent* acts of choosing, or positioning, or of experiencing the self as agentic. Such acts do not spring from an essential prediscursive self but rather are constituted in humanist discourses through which subjects (mis)take themselves to be "choosing," "positioning," etc. The terms "positioning," "choice," and "agency" can only be correctly used to describe what subjects do, Jones argues, by students who acknowledge that they are writing humanist discourse and not poststructuralist discourse.

The problematic relationship between the subject as it is constituted through humanist discourses and the subject as it is understood through poststructuralist discourses is one I have explored in detail. I do not set up a binary between the humanist subject and the "anti-humanist subject" (as Jones does in her article) but in part use poststructuralist theory to show how the humanist self is so convincingly achieved, and goes on being achieved, through the inscription of humanist discourses on the one who is *always already* a subject (Althusser, 1984), and who manages indeed to become "what will always already have been" (Lacan, 1966).

The *point* of poststructuralism is not to destroy the humanist subject nor to create its binary other, the "anti-humanist subject" (whatever that might be), but to enable us to see the subject's fictionality, while recognizing how powerful fictions are in constituting what we take to be real. One of Foucault's major contributions has been to enable us to see that what we understand by "being human" has shifted radically over the ages. His concern was not with individual subjects but with subjectification. At the same time, he was fascinated by the ways in which as writer he constituted himself as individual "author" (Foucault, 1977) even through the simple act of signing his

---

This chapter was originally published in *Gender and Education* 9(1) in 1997.

name to what he had written, rather than signing it as emerging from a particular discursive field. Deconstructive writing has been used by many writers in a complementary way to the writing of Foucault. The textual analysis it makes possible has enabled us to attend to the ways in which language traps us, for example, into binary forms of thought (such as the "humanist" and the "anti-humanist" subject). Deconstruction enables us to see that which we normally disattend, not just in the words on the page, but in the texts of "self" that signify this or that kind of individual subject. Poststructuralist theory draws attention to:

> [T]he signifying matter, which, instead of making itself transparent as it conveys a particular meaning, becomes somewhat opaque like a piece of stained or faceted glass. Thus in the most basic way the reader is invited to look *at* rather than *through* the linguistic surface. (Levine, 1991, p. xvi)

By looking "*at* rather than *through* the linguistic surface" we can begin to explore how it is that we can think we have, and act as if we have (and can be required by law to have), a sense of agency, and recognize at the same time that it is in the constitutive force of discourse that agency lies. Deconstructive thought thus requires us to take on board contradictory thoughts and to hold them together at the same time. In Chapter 4, on agency, I redefined agency as lying in the inscription of some forms of the humanist self (if you are constituted as a powerful agent you may well be able to act powerfully) *and,* more significant, as lying in the reflexive awareness of the constitutive power of language that becomes possible through poststructuralist theory. I have struggled to reclaim this concept for use in poststructuralist theory precisely because, as a feminist, I am not willing to forgo the possibility of conceptualizing and bringing about change. And as a poststructuralist I do not find that problematic. Linear forms of logic are too constraining for those of us who wish to embrace the rich complexity of life lived through multiple and contradictory discourses.

But for Jones, to talk of agency (she assumes rather than argues) is to insist on a real, prediscursive self. She is troubled by the tension between the constituted subject (which she acknowledges as "real") and the poststructuralist foregrounding of the discourse through which "subjects" are constituted. She argues that correct poststructuralist usage will be taken to have been achieved when: (a) the possibility of the humanist subject cannot be read into the text produced, and in its place an "anti-humanist" subject is achieved, and (b) it is understood, following Derrida, "that we cannot reach outside language; that everything is mediated by language and meaning" (Jones, 1997, pp. 264–65).

In relation to the first of these requirements, of course the writer is not in control of how the reader brings the written text to life in the reading of it. Reading and writing are deeply interactive processes, and readers will necessarily bring with them to any reading a range of strategies for making meaning out of the marks on the page. For some readers these may well be humanist strategies, and no amount of clever writing will dislodge them. It is this problem that I began work on in *Frogs and Snails* (Davies, 1989a).

In relation to the second of her requirements, it is useful to look closely at what Derrida meant by his famous phrase "il n'ya pas de hors-texte" ("there's nothing outside the text"). This can be taken to mean that the only thing we can legitimately attend to or talk about is language (or text), *or* it can be seen to mean that everything is text—that we are inseparable from the texts through which we are constituted and through which we constitute ourselves. In this reading *there can be no outside*. In other words, we can refuse the binary text/not-text, and see all as text. Fuery's (1995, p. 58) analysis of Derrida's meaning is that

> [N]othing can exist "outside" the text because the ideas of "outsides" and "centres" are problematic issues in their own right. . . . Textuality consumes all, because in attempting to represent or attribute meaning to something we textualize it. So the act of reading itself becomes part of the text. However, "reading" is not simply an act anybody might take up; rather, it is the site of a conflict as to who looks, that is, who is authorised to gaze and so has the capacity to read. The act of reading, then, comes to be determined through the act of interpretation.

Reading Derrida's words in this way, and thinking about the paper written by Jones as generating a site of conflict, her argument can be read as a claim that I and her students should not be authorized to gaze (at poststructuralist theory), as we do not have the capacity to read/write it. She then elaborates what a correct reading of poststructuralist theory is, proffering Butler as having appropriate authority.

For me this creates an intriguing puzzle. How does she make and sustain this claim? How is she reading my texts and the texts the students create in such a way that she sees the need to deauthorize us?

The "subject" of poststructuralist theory

The original writers of "poststructuralist theory" do not always name themselves as such. The writer, for example, whose work is perhaps most drawn on by those who name themselves poststructuralist is Foucault, yet Foucault himself expressed a wish to distance himself from the label. This is not uncommon when a new theoretical discursive field is being developed. The naming of it, the delineation of its subject matter, and the decision as to which authors to include in the discursive field being defined are not necessarily the same processes as those being undertaken by the writers being recognized. So there are those whose thinking inspires others, who in turn define and delimit what the field is that they are examining. In looking to what the original inspirational writers have to say about the human subject, we can then contemplate what sense we might want to make of the human subject in what we call "poststructuralist theory."

The original writers did not want to abandon the human subject, though they made that subject problematic. Foucault (1983, pp. 208–209) claimed that the goal of his work was to make sense of how "human beings are made subjects," not in the particularity of the lives of individual subjects, but in the processes that shift the meaning of being a subject over time:

> I would like to say, first of all, what has been the goal of my work during the last twenty years. It has not been to analyze the phenomena of power, nor to elaborate the foundations of such an analysis. My objective, instead, has been to create a history of the different modes by which, in our culture, human beings are made subjects. . . . Thus it is not power, but the subject, which is the general theme of my research.

Derrida is equally clear about the importance of the subject in his work. The subject, he says, is incontrovertibly there, as an *effect* of subjectivity. His interest, though, is in resituating the subject, in moving from a supposed identity that has substance independent of language to the subject inscribed in language:

> I have never said that the subject should be dispensed with. Only that it should be deconstructed. To deconstruct the subject does not mean to deny its existence. There are subjects, "operations" or "effects" (*effets*) of subjectivity. This is an incontrovertible fact. To acknowledge this does not mean, however, that the subject is what it says it is. The subject is not some meta-linguistic substance or identity, some pure cogito of self-presence; it is always inscribed in language. My work does not, therefore, destroy the subject; it simply tries to resituate it. (Derrida, in Kearney, 1994, p. 125)

And as Butler (1992, p. 4) herself comments, refusing the subject as a starting point for theorizing does not mean we can dispense with it altogether:

> To refuse to assume . . . a notion of the subject from the start is not the same as negating or dispensing with such a notion altogether; on the contrary, it is to ask after the process of its construction and the political meaning and consequentiality of taking the subject as a requirement or presupposition of theory.

It is assumed by poststructuralist theorists that the subject is *always already* a discursively constituted subject when s/he encounters the discursive possibilities of poststructuralism. What the encounter with poststructuralism does is to enable the subject to see not just the object it appears to itself to have become, but to see the ongoing and constitutive force of language (with all its contradictions). It is through making that constitutive force visible that the subject can see its "self" *as* discursive process, rather than as a unique relatively fixed personal invention. Poststructuralist discourse entails a move from the self as a noun (and thus stable and relatively fixed) to the self as a verb, always in process, taking its shape in and through the discursive possibilities through which selves are made. The "maker," in this poststructuralist turn, is what would appear to lie at the heart of the difference Jones is arguing between herself/Butler and me/her students. The maker, for Jones/Butler, is language. For me, it is not some prediscursive self, as Jones assumes, but an already discursively constituted subject, a subject in process, a subject as verb, a subject who, like poststructuralist writers, can learn to:

- see the constitutive process;

- read the texts of their "selving";

- recognize the constitutive power of discourses to produce historically located ideas of what it might even mean to be a self, or engage in "selving";

- look at the contradictions between discourses (and not reject them solely on those grounds); and

- play endlessly with the discursive possibilities that have been made observable through poststructuralist analysis.

As Mellor and Patterson (1996, p. 51) comment:

While modern linguistics is sometimes referred to as announcing the "death of the subject," it can be argued, as Foucault (1973) does in *The Order of Things,* that on the contrary, it marks the birth of a modern conception of the subject in which subjectivity is both the effect of "structures" *and* the ground where this effect will be opened to reflexive knowledge and seen through.

The subject of poststructuralism, unlike the humanist subject, then, is constantly in process; it only exists as process; it is revised and (re)presented through images, metaphors, storylines, and other features of language, such as pronoun grammar; it is spoken and re-spoken, each speaking existing in a palimpsest with the others. What Jones draws our attention to is that in attempting to reconceptualize the subject as process, we are limited by the images and metaphors we can find to create the new idea. Pronoun grammar is a good example of this. We cannot yet see how to do without it. We see the power of gendered pronouns, for example, to reconstitute the male/female binary every time we speak. We are frustrated to observe pronoun grammar re-creating the binary in the very language we use in our attempts to move beyond gender. Similarly, "I," which signals "identity," almost inevitably appears in the very same sentences we use to attempt to undo the idea of identity. Some poststructuralist writers adopt "i" to signal the shift they are attempting to engage in. But the text/discourse relentlessly writes us as existing, even when our intention is to enable the reader to disattend the active subject/writer and to attend to the constitutive force of discourse.

Palimpsest, a metaphor frequently used in poststructuralist writing, is equally problematic. This metaphor is derived from the image of writing on parchment, writing that was only partially erased to make way for new writing, each previous writing, therefore, bumping into and shaping the reading of the next layer of writing. This metaphor is used to explain the ways in which the subject is written and overwritten through multiple and contradictory discourses. It enables us to imagine, for example, how the unitary, essential, prediscursive self, constructed through humanist discourses, is still there as one amongst many writings, bumping into and shaping our interpretation of the self-as-process. At the same time, the concept of palimpsest holds the possibility of a conceptual trap. Since the image it may evoke is one in which the *original* writing is on a blank parchment, the metaphor of palimpsest can, without the writer or reader realizing it, hold in place the idea that there is an original prediscursive self, a humanist self, that is shaped through discourse. The semiotics of the palimpsest metaphor, however, enable us to imagine the humanist self not as one amongst many acts of writing but as the page itself. Because the blank parchment can be imagined as visible if we were to rub out all the writing, the prediscursive self who is free of discourses and able therefore to choose freely amongst discourses can be said to be "there" in the metaphor. Nothing can prevent a reader who wants to from reading the metaphor as incorrect in poststructuralist terms.

The intention of those who use the palimpsest metaphor is not to invite this reading. Its power as a conceptual tool requires a focus on the multiple layers of writing as they are written and erased and their effect on one another in the reading of them. Foucault works hard to persuade the reader to abandon the binary of surface/depth and to imagine surface as infinitely folded and containing its own depth. Yet a reader who interprets using binary strategies can read something behind the surface, which they take to be parchment, or prediscursive self, and the meanings the poststructuralist writer is struggling after are lost.

At the same time, any writer using the concepts of palimpsest and surfaces can continue to point out that selving or subjectification can be understood in the intricate folds of reading and writing and that the parchment should not (mistakenly) be equated with either an imagined original self or the body. This is precisely the kind of work that Butler does in her discussion of the metaphor of self as performance. She makes clear that the poststructuralist subject is expressed (formed) in the very act of the performance and does not exist independent of the performance. At the same time, she carefully explains the dangers of her metaphor if it brings to mind the actor (self) who acts many parts and who is identifiably separate from the part that is being played. Curiously, her warning both is and is not accepted by Jones. While she says "performance" unacceptably invokes the performer behind the performance, she incorporates "performance" into her repertoire of acceptable poststructuralist terminology.

Structuralism and poststructuralism

One reading of the argument that Jones makes is that the difference between Jones/Butler and Davies/the students lies in the different possible readings of the relations between structuralism and poststructuralism. Her reading of the relationship is that the determinism of structuralism is still there, in poststructuralist theorizing, but it has moved from structures to discourses. My reading has been different. While I have centered discourse, and recognized its constitutive force, I have read subjects as both constituted and constitutive. Indeed, in reviewing my earliest attempts at poststructuralist writing, I find I took the fundamental difference between structuralism and poststructuralism to be the active taking up of discourse as one's own that poststructuralist theory made visible, and the room for movement that the reflexively aware subject had once the constitutive power of discourses was made visible. I was fascinated by the ways in which the contradictory readings of myself, made so problematic within humanist theory, could become extraordinary resources for exploring the complex and dynamic relations between subjects and the discourses through which they were constituted.

Interestingly, I have found no two accounts that are in agreement on the precise difference between structuralism and poststructuralism. This is, of course, predictable given the diversity of writings pulled together under the label "poststructuralism," and given that "poststructuralism [has] openly sought out and celebrated the inconclusive nature of its own methodologies" (Fuery, 1995, p. 15). The reading Jones produces of the difference is as legitimate a reading as any other. However, the difference can also be read as Fuery (1995, p. 38) reads it:

> Part of the reason why post-structuralism is designated "post" is that it claims to have superseded structuralism by challenging two of its foundational claims. One is that structures are present in all spheres of human activity (from anthropology to economics to religion) and that by understanding such structures we gain a sense of "truth." The other claim is that the structure of the sign . . . is the systemic key to all processes of meaning and communication. Post-structuralism challenges these two concepts on the grounds that there can be no truth or truths . . . outside the construction of [them]; . . . furthermore, it is imperative not only to reveal the artifices of such social structures but also to develop a more dynamic model of the sign.

In other words, for Fuery, the important difference is that poststructuralism *rejects* structuralism's absolute certainties. Instead, it takes up and plays with the idea that any truth is constructed (presumably including structuralist and poststructuralist truths), and it seeks a dynamic (rather than a deterministic) understanding of the way signs/discourses work. Fuery also points out that that dynamism is inherent in poststructuralism itself: "The folds of post-structuralism—subjectivity, signification, culture, power, self-reflexive analysis, and, of course, desire—can never be contained comfortably within any structure or system" (p. 1).

Jones, in contrast, appears to seek certainties—a certain "truth" about poststructuralism. And she finds in her students' and in my writing a form of words that stand outside that truth.

What is curious, in examining her text, however, is the similarity between the words the students use and the words Jones uses to describe those same students in their partial take-up of poststructuralist theory. In their own words, they "take things up with alacrity" or find a subject position "produced as an impossibility" (Jones, 1997, p. 266). They imagine themselves being "multiply positioned," offered "numerous subject positions," actively taking up "different subjectivities," seeing that they "might take on different, even contradictory, subjectivities. . . ." Jones writes of them as equally active in their relations with discourse: they "struggle with its meanings," they "baulk at" it, even though they have "learned to question," "to see," to "become critical," "to understand," and they "encounter [certain ideas] with suspicion" and "adopt" discursive frameworks (pp. 261, 262, 263, 264, 268). The students thus constituted in this writing certainly do not seem to confirm Butler's claim that "There is only the taking up of the tools where they lie, where the very 'taking up' is enabled by the tool lying there" (Butler, 1990, p. 145, emphasis added by Jones). Jones engages in an analysis of her own students that shows how the taking up of poststructuralist tools is not enabled simply by them lying there. There are other tools needed (such as structuralism) and, according to Jones, there are other (humanist) tools getting in the way, having their constitutive effects, occluding the perception of the thing lying there, preventing it from taking the student over.

Is Jones saying indirectly, through her choice of words, that she does not agree with Butler, and that she now prefers to engage in humanist analyses? On this point I am not clear. However, she does appear to unequivocally claim the active subject (acting upon discourse) as incompatible with post-structuralist theory. Of course, Jones is not alone in this reading of post-structuralism. There are other readers who define it as ruling out altogether the possibility of a speaking subject. But as Hazel (1996, p. 315) observes in response to one such reader:

> I see no impossible conflict between the practice of a politics of voice and the critical examination of its ground; . . . "the experiencing subject" that we all feel ourselves to be and for whom we seek acknowledgment, is not something that can easily be comprehended . . . [and] despite the relationship we inevitably retain to the humanist subject, this [comprehension] is not an unproblematic goal for feminism.

And Flax (1993, pp. 92–93) argues, even more strongly, that emancipatory struggle and the poststructuralist subject not only can but must go conceptually hand in hand:

> Many theorists argue that the decentered/postmodernist forms of subjectivity some critics advocate as replacements for older ones cannot exercise the agency required for liberatory political activity. Are the claims of the Enlightenment philosophers from Kant to Habermas correct? Does emancipatory action—and the very idea and hope of emancipation—depend upon the development of a unitary self capable of autonomy and undetermined self-reflection? Can there be forms of subjectivity that are simultaneously fluid, multicentered, and effective in the "outer" worlds of political life and social relations? Could multicentered and overdetermined subjects recognize relations of domination and struggle to overcome them? I believe a unitary self is unnecessary, impossible, and a dangerous illusion. Only multiple subjects can invent ways to struggle against domination that will not merely recreate it.

Poststructuralist pedagogy

Jones observes that the students' understanding of poststructuralist theory is inadequate because it is contaminated by their selves already constituted through other discourses. What puzzles me is that their attempts are not welcomed as a stepping-off stone that the students can use to explore reflexively the ways in which they are constituted as subjects through these conflicting discourses. One of the major difficulties in introducing poststructuralist theory to students is to make language reflexively visible, that is, not just visible as an object, but visible as an active force shaping bodies, shaping desire, shaping perception. In my own experience of teaching, the words of poststructuralist theory are not enough. The students have to be able to catch language in the act of shaping subjectivities. An examination of their own writing, or of their own storytelling, or of their own acts of reading can be ideal means by which they can begin to catch the text in the act of constituting (Davies, 1993, 1996a).

The pedagogical intent of Jones for students who engage with poststructuralist discourse would seem to be, in the final event, that they use it "correctly," rather than that they develop the reflexive awareness and competencies that enable them to engage with the possibilities poststructuralism can open up. She wants them, in other words, to become competent mimics. She is afraid they have become incompetent to the extent that they are mimicking the wrong person and thus muddling their discourses, using "positioned" when they should use "produced" (Jones, 1997, pp. 263, 265, 268). Of course, it is always partially true that what we require of our students is that they learn to mimic the discourses we want them to be able to use (Davies, 1996b). Crane (1995, pp. ix–x) talks of the dilemma this creates for students who are simultaneously required to be original and to become "imposters":

> As a student, I've always hated brownnosers. As a teacher . . . , I've also hated them, but only when they've been too "obvious"; that is, when their performance is too easily seen, when their interest in me as a teacher is not "personal," but an act, false, an imposture—which may mean that it seems too personal. Yet (true) imposture—unlike impersonation—can't be seen too easily. An imposter, after all, relies on acting and seeming genuine, and that label only really fits after the ingenuity of the act—that blurring of false and true—has been revealed.

It would seem that both Jones and I want our students to become competent in their use of poststructuralist discourse, though Jones suggests it may indeed be too hard for many students. She also claims she does not mind "which discursive framework" her students "adopt" (Jones, 1997, p. 268). (I am sure she does mind, actually. I cannot imagine her cheerfully reading an essay using the discursive framework of members of the Ku Klux Klan, for example, and complimenting the student on how well s/he had taken up the discourse of that group.) She does not mind, she says, as long as they understand that they cannot use (some) active verbs, such as "the subject who positions herself" (p. 269), or who chooses, or who struggles after the possibility of agency, and at the same time claim to be using poststructuralist theory. Students must take a pure line in which all signs of an active, individual subject are removed if they want to claim to be using poststructuralist theory. For me, this sounds worryingly like the correct knowledge of Parsons or Marx or the Bible that students have been required to achieve in the past. Both feminist pedagogy and poststructuralist pedagogy can be less authoritarian and less absolute in their strategies, and thus have quite different effects.

In my own teaching I do not want my students to become mimics of what they take poststructuralism to be, producing forgeries of "correct" "anti-humanist" experiencing of "themselves" (though I have no doubt some of them will do that). Rather, what I want of them is to learn the skills of finding the texts/discourses they interact with in the act of shaping them and shaping what they see. When these are humanist texts, I want them in particular to be able to see that process, to see why they find those texts desirable and pleasurable, and why the text of themselves as humanist subjects is so hard to eradicate from their writing. At the same time, I want them to experience the disruptive/blissful possibilities opened up through the play of poststructuralist practices (Davies, 1994). This requires a particular way of attending to the details of the texts they read and see and hear and the texts they produce (which includes the texts of themselves). The skills of attending to texts in poststructuralist ways are ones that must be struggled after continuously; they are not achievable as a repertoire of specific skills, though there are ways of writing and speaking that are helpful in producing poststructuralist practices.

> When people follow Foucault, when they're fascinated by him, it's because they're doing something with him, in their own work, in their own independent lives. It's not just a question of intellectual understanding or agreement, but of intensity, resonance, musical harmony. (Deleuze, 1995, p. 86)

What seems most powerful to me in poststructuralist theory is precisely the fact that we are taken up/over/under by contradictory discursive practices. As humanists we can engage in quite extraordinary intellectual feats to convince ourselves of our unitariness. As feminists we can use the confusion to sharpen our reflexive gaze and resist our take-up in discourses we find undesirable. As poststructuralists we can find the ways in which the "injunction to be a given gender takes place" (Butler, 1990, p. 145). What I encourage my students to do is to take up the possibilities inherent in the complex reconfigurations poststructuralist theory makes possible, and to find where that might take them (Davies et al., 1997). For those who do so, they may well find themselves irreversibly traversed and shaken by new discourses. It is that shaking up that is so fascinating (and sometimes dangerous) for students of poststructuralism:

Lacan wants us, his readers (his analysands?), to be challenged and changed intellectually through his seminars and writings. This is because at the heart of things, as with the poststructuralist movement overall (if one can speak of it in such terms), is the need to analyse analysis, understand understanding, interpret interpretation. And once such a task is undertaken, one of the consequences is a self-reflexivity that must challenge the very discursive practices in operation. (Fuery, 1995, pp. 9–10)

And classrooms, after all, are also sites of struggle, struggles that are about existence and about power. I do not believe it is appropriate, or even useful, as a pedagogical strategy to declare that the familiar sense of self the students have achieved is not only *sous rature* (under erasure), but that it simply does not exist *while we are engaging in poststructuralist discourse.* To put something under erasure is to say that it is *a term we still need and use,* but one that needs deconstructing and moving beyond. To enable students to move confidently beyond the humanist conception of the subject, students need familiar ground from which to speak and write. The texts of their own speaking and writing can then become the material that they use to acquire the skills of deconstruction. The complexity of this task should not be underestimated, however, and if students need some aspects of familiar discourses in order to continue as speaking, writing subjects while they find their deconstructive feet, then it is important to ensure that they have easy (and eventually reflexively aware) access to them.

~

What follows as the final chapter in this book is a paper I wrote with Cath Laws, a friend and PhD student of mine. What we have done in this paper is to work together with the data she has collected in the school of which she is principal to further explore the questions raised in this paper and to extend the examination of power and powerlessness begun in Chapter 7, "Classroom competencies and marginal positionings." We are also interested in the question of whether poststructuralist theory can be used to inform practice as we believe it can, rather than leading, as some assert, to amoral forms of inaction. We are fascinated by the use of poststructuralist theory in Cath's practice as a tool that guides the reflexive unfolding of a different way of practicing being principal and researcher.

9 ~ Poststructuralist theory in practice: Working with "behaviorally disturbed" children

IN A RECENTLY PUBLISHED COLLECTION of articles focusing on the "relativism/realism debate" (Parker, 1998), a frequent claim was made by those who saw themselves as "realists" that no matter how convincing the arguments of poststructuralists and other "relativists" might be, psychologists committed to action have no choice but to retain their realist "truths." Some of the "realist" authors went so far as to claim that "relativists" were immoral because they were incapable of action or commitment. In her response to these articles Bronwyn argued, amongst other things, that poststructuralist insights can be powerfully linked to action (Davies, 1998). In this chapter we extend that argument, using the work that Cath has been engaged in for the last two years, as poststructuralist researcher and as principal in a school for "behaviorally disturbed" children. We will show, in detail, how poststructuralist theory can work in relation to practice.

The skepticism about the usefulness of poststructuralist theory has recently extended into the field of behavioral disorders. *Behavioral Disorders* is a key journal for those working with students positioned as having behavioral problems/difficulties/disorders/disturbance. In a recent special issue (Kauffman, 1998a) there were no less than six articles on "postmodernism." Even though the authors do not use the term "poststructuralism" in the articles, it is clear that the term "postmodernism" is used by them as an overarching term that includes poststructuralism and the processes of deconstruction. The editor, James Kauffman, opened the series of articles with an extraordinary level of ambivalence saying that "if postmodernism is an idea, not merely a word pretending to be an idea, then its consequences could be substantial" (Kauffman, 1998b, p. 149). But what, he asks, is the definition of this idea, for without the definition, the consequences for postmodernism can only be minimal. He wonders whether there might be a "real postmodernism" and "faux postmodernism" (p. 150).

This chapter was written with Cath Laws and was originally published in the *International Journal for Qualitative Studies in Education* in 1999.

Elkind's (1998) article is the only one in this collection that seriously supports postmodernism. Then Edgar (1998, p. 161) responds to Elkind, suggesting that postmodern thought has made him less absolute in his judgments:

> The good old days seemed better. We all knew what we believed (and it was right). . . . Those days are gone, forever, I hope. First of all we were not right. (If we had been we would not be having this discussion about Behavior Disorders.) Second, I no longer want to be a zealot about anything. I was a zealot in the old days. I believed behaviorism could cure any disability. With my colleagues I shouted down dissent, and our world view won. We had our day the in the sun, and it didn't work! Not that all the ideas were wrong, but the notion that we had all the answers for every problem was wrong.

Edgar acknowledges postmodernists for opening his eyes to multiple narratives but rejects what he attributes as the postmodernist notion that there can be no common narratives. This is a rather startling mode of dismissal. A central interest of postmodernist/poststructuralist theorists working in the field of education is to explore common narratives, the way people use the socially available repertoire of storylines to tie the elements of their existence together into "meaningful" continuities (Davies, 1991, Chapter 4; Haug et al., 1987). Children come to read the myriad of arbitrary signifiers—the words, gestures, objects—with which they are surrounded in such a way that arbitrariness is banished and meanings, conventions, and truths are established (Walkerdine, 1988). We read the attempts to understand how this is done as central to poststructuralist thought.

The debate about the usefulness of poststructuralism also occurs within the field of those who would describe themselves as "poststructuralists." Jones (1997), for example, is critical of what she sees as the recurring presence of the humanist subject in writing that claims to be poststructuralist. She regards words such as "agency" and "choice" (Davies, 1991; Davies and Harré, 1990; Chapters 4 and 5, this volume) or "performance" (Butler, 1993) as signaling the (theoretically unacceptable) presence of a prediscursive or essential self. Poststructuralist theory is declared by Jones to be unable to theorize anything other than the oppressive forces of subjection: any active take-up by human subjects of the power they are subjected by is outside the bounds of poststructuralist theorizing. We take this to be a troubling but predictable misreading of poststructuralist theory, and it is one we will address in this chapter.

The dual nature of subjectification is hard to grasp: one is simultaneously subjected and at the same time can become an agentic, speaking subject. The speaking/writing subject can go beyond the intentions of powerful others and beyond the meanings of the discourses through which they are subjected while *necessarily and at the same time* being dependent on their successful subjection for becoming someone who can speak/write meaningfully and convincingly beyond the terms of their subjection. To grasp this requires a capacity to think outside our more practiced, linear patterns of thought. We wish to claim the concepts of agency and performance and to use them in a poststructuralist framework to make sense of the ways in which we are at the same time shaped by forces external to us, and yet through that very shaping gain the possibility of power and of agency:

> Power acts on the subject in at least two ways: first, as what makes the subject possible, the condition of its possibility and its formative occasion, and second, as what is taken up and reiterated in the subject's own acting. As a subject *of* power (where "of" connotes both "belonging to" and "wielding"), the subject eclipses the conditions of its own emergence; it eclipses power with power. . . . [T]he subject emerges both as the *effect* of a prior power and as the *condition of possibility* for a radically conditioned form of agency. (Butler, 1997, p. 14)

In this chapter we will explore the ways in which subjects are formed, or made possible, and also the ways in which they come to eclipse the conditions of their own emergence. In the case of the boys in this study, such an eclipse is made almost impossible because of the very nature of their subjection.

Burman (1994) identifies psychological discourses themselves, and in particular developmental psychology, as powerful formative discourses through which students are subjected. Indeed, psychology has been described as a major tool for the classification, surveillance, and shaping of those without power (Rose, 1985) or, as we will show, for constituting subjects who can have no access to legitimate forms of power or agency. As Walkerdine (1989) has shown, it can be argued that psychological thinking, psychology as a science, contributes to the conditions that produce taken-for-granted practices, which in turn produce taken-for-granted "facts." Those psychological discourses that seek to measure, categorize, and plot the normalcy/abnormalcy of children and adults are explored in this paper as they produce, arguably, not only subjects, but also the obviousness, even inevitability, of the subjects' "condition." What might agency look like for subjects so shaped, for the "behaviorally disturbed" students who are defined as somehow having escaped their subjection?

Doing/being a "good school student"

The great majority of children are readily able to recognize what is meant by "good school behavior" and they take up, for the most part, the behaviors consistent with this meaning. The question usually asked about "behaviorally disturbed" children is, how is it that these children do not take up these behaviors? It is generally assumed by those asking such questions that there is some fault in them that they do not voluntarily take them up.

The coercive practices through which most children are persuaded to take up the practices of being a "good student" are themselves largely invisible to those with the power to coerce. The following text records an incident in a regular/mainstream high school. It took the teachers by surprise when they were presented with it in written form. They had not noticed the incident happening at the time and were unhappy that Bronwyn had noticed it and chosen to record it:

> Another moment. We walk into the staff room. There is a boy standing against the wall in the corridor outside. Another boy speaks to him and a teacher says loudly, "You are not to speak to him. He is not to be spoken to." Over an hour later we come out of the staff room. The boy is sitting on the floor against the wall with his head bowed. As we walk past he pulls off his baseball cap and bursts into tears. One of the teachers says "I've never seen you do that before" and we walk on. Apart from this comment our silence suggests that his presence in the corridor is utterly normal within the context of schools. We presume he has seriously transgressed the school rules (quite possibly a rule that requires adult-like behavior from him, such as respect for others' rights) and so we, like all the other teachers, file past him on our way out of the staff room, seeing him and not speaking to him or about him. I feel sick in my collusion as I too walk past him. In large part I say nothing because it seems that to everyone else it is a normal event. It must seem normal to the boy too, because there is nothing actually holding him there, sobbing in the corridor, except his reading of the authority relations of the school. There are no tangible chains yet he does not see himself as having a viable alternative to his moment of shame? despair? in the corridor. (Davies, 1996a, p. 30)

As Foucault (1988, p. 42) observes of the ancient Romans engaging in penitence: "The acts by which he punishes himself are indistinguishable from the acts by which he reveals himself. . . . Penance is not nominal, but dramatic. To prove suffering, to show shame, to make visible humility and exhibit modesty—these are the main features of punishment." And so it is in school: The school hands the boy his chance to perform his punishment and he takes it up with evident pain and a display of competent knowledge in how the receipt of punishment must be achieved, including the display of "genuine" despair. This is what Butler (1997, p. 113) refers to as the "paradox of how the very possibility of subject formation depends upon a passionate pursuit of a recognition which . . . [can be] inseparable from condemnation."

We include this story at the beginning of this discussion to remind ourselves, and our readers, that schools work hard to shape students and that the processes involved are not necessarily benign (they may even be regarded as violent), and that they are not achieved by active teachers working on passive students. The punishment would not work if the boy did not take it up as his own. At the same time, the meting out and taking up of such punishment is so taken for granted that it is virtually invisible. Most teachers and most principals on reading the story of the boy in the corridor are brought up short because it enables them to see differently practices that had become so much a part of the daily normality of school life that they no longer noticed them. We use this story as a framing device for the students in the stories that follow to show both how surprising it is that some children are not totally subjected by such training in "normality" and to make it clear that such training does take place: children do not necessarily take up "normality" through some benign process of osmosis. Even the boy who is reprimanded for speaking to the boy in the corridor must enter into a correct knowing of how to see and interact with the act of punishment. He may well take up as his own the shame of the boy's performance of punishment and resolve not to find himself in such a situation.

In humanist discourse, the primary discourse through which teachers interact with students, each person has an obligation to take themselves up as a knowable, recognizable identity who speaks for themselves and who accepts responsibility for their actions. Such responsibility is understood as resting on a moral base and entailing personal commitment to the moral position implied in their choices (Davies, 1991, Chapter 4). Central to the "good school behavior" discourse is the notion that each child freely "chooses" to get it right. In doing so it is understood that they believe that they do have choice, and that they must be seen to be making this choice, again and again.

Social practices in schools are discursively regulated by the production of "truths" and "knowledges" about children. The take-up of such "truths" as applying to oneself (as student, as teacher) are powerful because that take-up is precisely what regulates citizens in the democratic order (Walkerdine, 1988). The scientific "truth" about children's reasoning (and, in this context, how they reason about behavior) is a powerful tool in pedagogic practices. By producing a truth about "natural reason," a quality that individuals take up and that enables them to choose to act appropriately (thus bringing about for themselves the good "consequences" of getting it right), the government of reason and of reasonable people is assured (Walkerdine, 1988).

Both "choice" and the closely related concept "consequences" are central to the "good school behavior" discourse. They are used by teachers and students to "manage" classroom order. But this management of order cannot be achieved by teachers' efforts alone. Students must take up as their own a desire for the sort of order the teacher wants: classroom order can only be achieved through an active collaboration between teachers and students. While such work on the part of students is usually ignored by teachers, it can be shown that students actively work to cue in to the particular form of order desired by each of their teachers, and through their mode of action and interaction bring this form of order into being. Both teachers and students develop a detailed knowledge of their classrooms in order to present themselves as competent members of that particular scene (Davies, 1983; Davies and Hunt, 1994).

Children take on very quickly the repertoires that are available to them to be "good school students." Many of them can articulate the overt, and even the more hidden, rules about appropriate school behavior. Most take on the patterns that are required of them by the particular adult with whom they are interacting. The boy in the corridor may have transgressed earlier in the day, but now he sits in the corridor working hard at being obedient to the authority of the school. His task, and the task of all students, is to show a commitment to maintaining the scene the way the teachers want it. This may involve not only accepting the teachers' right to define and to punish unacceptable behavior, but also collaborating to bring recalcitrant students into line: the words "You are not to speak to him, he is not to be spoken to" instantly re-formed the collaborative silence around the boy in the corridor. Through such collaboration students in particular can legitimize their own claims to competent membership of the classroom (Davies and Munro, 1987). As Butler (1997, pp. 118–19) observes in her analysis of Althusser's writing on the process by which one becomes subject, the idea of the bad or unformed subject is the starting point of subjection: each person has to constantly achieve themselves as "not bad" in order to be recognized as an acceptably formed subject:

> To become a "subject" is thus to have been presumed guilty, then tried and declared innocent. Because this declaration is not a single act but a status incessantly reproduced, to become a "subject" is to be continuously in the process of acquitting oneself of the accusation of guilt. It is to have become an emblem of lawfulness, a citizen in good standing, but one for whom that status is tenuous, indeed, one who has known—somehow, somewhere—what it is *not* to have that standing and hence to have been cast out as guilty. Yet because this guilt conditions the subject, it constitutes the prehistory of the subjection to the law by which the subject is produced. Here one might usefully conjecture that the reason there are so few references to "bad subjects" in Althusser is that the term tends towards the oxymoronic. To be "bad" is not yet to be a subject, not yet to have acquitted oneself of the allegation of guilt.

In regular/mainstream school settings, students are taught that they have choices about how to behave, and that their own recognizability as credible and competent students will depend on learning to make the right choices.

They are coached in these right choices. Being recognized as a legitimate or "competent" student requires being read as one who knows when to work, how to learn, when to be creative (and in what contexts), when to speak and what can be spoken, and when to be silent (Kamler, Maclean, Reid, and Simpson, 1993). Such regulated behavior on the part of students is understood, in teaching and learning discourses, to be necessary for teachers to be able to teach. Walkerdine (1990, p. 21) talks about this regulation as a mimicry of "scientific process" in which the school room is a laboratory where "development could be watched, monitored and set along the right path."

This commitment to regulating classrooms relies on the idea of choice. Walkerdine (1989) sees this type of choice as an illusion, but an illusion that is key to what is taken to be correct classroom life. We come to believe that schooling involves a freedom to choose, through observing "choices" taking place. As teachers we position ourselves and the students within discourses that entail the making of choices. This consistent positioning creates an appearance for self and others that the choices made are a feature of each person rather than of educational discourses (Davies, 1991, Chapter 4). Thus choosing to do good behavior in school makes a "good student" and a "good child"—and a "good person," that is, one who recognizably "knows" how to behave and does so willingly.

One of the powerful tools that teachers use to persuade children to take up the practices involved in "good school behavior" and in turn to contribute to the democratic order is the notion of "consequences." This idea is grounded in the scientific discourse that every action has an equal and opposite reaction. Every action we perform has a reaction—every behavior has a consequence. Every appropriate behavior has a positive consequence. Every inappropriate behavior has a negative consequence.

It is the responsibility of teachers to have children learn about consequences and, in setting up the conditions for this learning, to design a range of consequences appropriate for school practices. From a range of behavior-management materials available for teachers these consequences include positive verbal and nonverbal responses (a smile, a nod, statements such as "well done"; stamps, stickers, award cards; desired activity rewards; prizes). Negative consequences include: verbal and nonverbal responses (a frown, statements such as "this is not your best work"); additional work; restrictions on participating in desired activities through detentions; being sent to other classrooms where other students see the student who is not getting it right; being sent to someone in a position of higher authority to "discuss" the "inappropriate behavior"; being sent to sit in the corridor where others can observe you as one who has got it wrong; being sent away from the school (suspension); being sent to another school (exclusion, referral to specialist units); being sent from schooling altogether (expulsion). The consequences and the practices of applying and regulating students help produce what it means to be a child at school—what behaviors are required to get it right at school—what it means to be not a child but a "student," and preferably a "good student."

The positive consequences are not freely given—students have to "earn" them. The behavioral-management discursive practices hold that there is danger in overrewarding students and students must come to rely on the more "intrinsic" rewards. Children must come to love and value learning and doing what is right for its own sake; that is, they must actively engage in becoming the subject being produced.

While most children take on the repertoires that are available to them to be "good school students," this should not be taken to indicate that this take-up is not extraordinarily complex. The available repertoires for being a "good school student" differ between classrooms and from one situation to another within classrooms. They differ between the classroom and the playground. And, further, they differ from one child to another. Repertoires are highly situation-specific. Being recognized as a good student entails correct performances of lining up, eating lunch, playing in a small space, playing in a large space—each of these in gender-specific ways. And, further, doing good behavior is not enough—sometimes you have to be funny and even on the edge of naughty to do the performances that are required for you to be recognized as a well-behaved student with an interesting personality—as being more than a mimic of what the teacher wants (Davies, 1996b). Then we have to add on the performances that are required to be accepted by other students, such as being a good friend to others; being someone other children admire; not getting others into trouble; liking/disliking the "right" kids; etc. Then there are the performances required for parent[s] and family members: not getting into too much trouble; not embarrassing older siblings; doing good schoolwork. But this complex repertoire of acceptable actions is not simply there for the observing and the take-up. It is necessary not only to achieve yourself as the person who *can be recognized* as one who *can* legitimately take up these behaviors, but also *to be recognized as actually* taking them up. The same behavior can be read as "genuine" and as fake, or even as inappropriate, depending on who the student is recognized as having become. Some of the complexity of this work is evident in the following scene in a mainstream primary school, recorded by the teachers involved in the unfolding story of these boys. It is interesting, too, to see the playing out of the choice/consequence discourse in this scenario:

> On the playground, Theo, Ned, Miles and Patrick are involved in a fight. Theo and Miles are on the ground rolling, hitting and punching each other. Ned is standing, kicking Miles. Patrick is watching. The fight is about the disappear-

ance of a lost plastic horse they have been playing with. They think that Miles has hidden it. The teacher sees the fight and calls for them to stop it. They don't stop and she has to intervene to pull them apart. Theo runs away and the other three continue the fight by throwing verbal abuse at each other. Several times they try to engage in physical fighting again.

[Interruption—the bell rings]

The students wait to talk to the teacher about the incident. While they wait, they discuss together a story they will deliver to the teacher. They have stopped fighting. Ned leads the others with the story line. (Another teacher observes this happening.)

[Interruption while they walk over to the teacher's room to discuss incident]

On the way to the teacher's room the students laugh with each other. They posture in surly ways towards the teacher when they arrive at the room. She tells them that they are obviously not ready to discuss the incident yet. She separates the students and leaves them to think about the incident. She speaks to them individually about their behavior. The consequences of the behavior are that they have reduced time on the playground the following day because they have to see the teacher before playing and convince her that they will play safely.

[Two days later]

Ned and Theo are walking down the corridor past the teacher who had intervened in their fight two days earlier. They speak pleasantly to her, saying "Hello, Paquita." She replies. The boys are followed by their own teacher who looks angry because they have just been very disruptive in her gym session. The students move down the corridor, embrace each other and sing to each other (not provocatively, but loud enough for the teacher to hear), "We are the naughty boys . . . " They continue down the corridor laughing.

[*The teachers, who are engaged in a poststructuralist analysis of their own practices, go on to write:*]

Here the boys display at least four kinds of competence. 1) They have been physically powerful in the playground, 2) they have got the better of the teacher in the gym, 3) they have behaved in a friendly and disarming way to Paquita (who might have taken it as a genuine step forward in her establishment of a good relationship with them in which they would become the sort of people she wanted them to become if she had not seen the next bit unfold as they went down the corridor). And finally 4) they have consolidated their friendship with each other around their knowledge of themselves as "the naughty boys." (Davies, 1996a, pp. 165–66)

Doing/being "disturbed"

What then of the children who do not "choose" to behave in the required ways and for whom no level of positive or negative consequences seems to be able to persuade them to do so? How is it that these children come to be positioned as "disturbed" in a developmental/categorizing psychological sense? Walkerdine (1988), in looking at mathematics learning, observes that correct accomplishment is the result of developing "understanding" and that failure is understood as being produced through a lack of requisite "experience" or "readiness." This does not seem to be the case in the area of behavior. There seems to be an age when inappropriate behavior is not tolerated, and when an argument about inexperience or lack of "readiness" will not be accepted by anyone. The school-age child is quickly positioned as having to get on appropriately with thirty other children. Failure to do so is initially viewed as lack of experience—did the student go to preschool?—did the student have time with others in child care?—is the student too immature for what is required from school? The gaze of a developmental/categorizing psychology constitutes women as mothers—and bad mothers if their children do not get it right at school. While the child is seen to be the one to be "worked on," the blame for this lack of appropriate school behavior is usually attributed to poor parenting—by mothers.

This way of interpreting students not doing the "right" thing usually lasts for about three months. By then it is expected that they will have the experiences required and should be ready. If they are not, then the focus is on specifically identifying the skills the child needs to have in school—the actual actions involved in the practices. These are then taught to students in social-skills training programs. If this is not successful then a developmental/categorizing psychological discourse is used to make sense of the failure, attributing the cause of failure to the child—rather than to the discourses at play, or to the context, or to the other players. And so these students come to be recognized as "disturbed." Their chance of being recognized as normal, let alone "good students" are at that point severely curtailed. The child's failure can be seen as one of not achieving the rational humanist self—the self who would automatically make good choices (Davies, 1991). Not to be seen to be in control of the self involves the irrational—and the irrational is read as disturbance.

The dominance of a developmental/categorizing psychological discourse in schools can be traced to the late nineteenth century, when the mind became a focus of investigation. At this time there was the simultaneous emergence of both the individual and the child as objects of social and scientific gaze. Burman (1994) sees modern psychology coming of age with the political utility of mental testing. The development of testing and the process of inquiry being used positioned psychology as a "science"—the science of the mental. Burman has proposed that investigation in a developmental/categorizing psychology has been structured by the technology of testing, measurement, and observation. Being able to classify, measure, and regulate populations that were a social threat to the prevailing order became important. With a notion of "standardized" testing and objectivity, the moral evaluation that underlies the description is rendered invisible through the apparent impartiality of statistical norms.

What is not made visible in such psychological analyses is the chaos and complexity of the research process. The complex disorder of individual development is transposed into orderly steps to maturity reflecting explicit social interests in maintaining social control within and between social groups and nations. The rise of modern psychology was produced to meet demands of prevailing social anxieties, such as ensuring the quality of the stock, inculcating good habits, and dealing with poverty and crime. A developmental/categorizing psychology fulfilled the middle-class desire to classify that which it did not understand and to bring it under surveillance in an attempt to control it (Burman, 1994).

Positioning children as objects of a developmental/categorizing psychological inquiry can lead to a failure to theorize the contexts they inhabit—and it can lead to individualistic interpretations of socially structured phenomenon. This leads inexorably to "victim blaming" and the behavior becomes that which is responsible for many of the social problems in the world. The current legislation in some countries, including Australia, that prohibits young people from gathering in groups on the street makes clear the way many young people are positioned as "dangerous to society." The students in Cath's school find themselves constituted through discourses in which they are seen to have a disability—a disturbance that often requires a "treatment" modality. The "treatment" requires them to experience more of the consequences and often in an extreme way.

There is an ambivalence about how to deal with such a thing as a "psychological disability" (another name given to behavioral disturbance) and whether there is such a thing at all. While some see "disability" purely in individual terms, children are most often not responded to as having a "disability" in the same way others have a disability, for example, a physical, sensory, or intellectual disability. Rather, they are perceived in terms of the threat to the fabric of society that their presence is assumed to carry with it. They threaten to undermine the power and control that teachers and principals perceive themselves to need for the smooth running of their schools.

They are also often perceived in terms of physical threat and the harm they may do to other students.

This reading of the students gives them interesting opportunities to display "power." The power is attributed to them on the assumption that they do know the right thing to do and that they are capable, unlike others, of choosing to ignore what is right and good. Going back to Butler's definition of agency, these students are assumed, in such a reading, to have been formed as others have been formed and to be seizing illegitimately a chance to "eclipse power with power" (Butler, 1997, p. 14):

> Shane was suspended from his regular school today. In assembly he was wearing his baseball cap. When he was asked to take it off, he refused—got up, turned his back on the principal, said nothing and walked out in front of a couple of hundred students. (Cath's journal)

Shane was suspended for this action. The action of "choosing" to ignore the power of the principal, of turning his back and walking out was too much for the school. "Consequences" were brought to bear and Shane was sent from the school. He must learn about consequences and so shape his actions accordingly.

Shane later told Cath that he had had his hair cut short and did not want it seen—but of course he could not say that at the time. To provide such an explanation in front of the assembly would be embarrassing. Further, to do such a thing was neither a recognizable pattern of behavior that he could imagine anyone taking up and it was certainly not one of the repertoires of action that he could take up and in doing so be recognized as behaving acceptably. So he walked out. An obvious choice, really, but it could not be read by the school this way. His action was read as powerful and disruptive. Staff at the school were extremely upset by his refusal to comply—and perhaps even a little afraid of what they saw as his challenge. They saw what he did as all the more extreme because it was, apparently, done without emotion. The display of correct emotions is a crucial aspect of being properly subjected, or as having taken up correctly the liberal humanist version of being a self.

The magnitude of the response to Shane's simple attempt to avoid embarrassment is based on a reading of his act as powerful and as disturbing. It is also based on an assumption that students such as Shane do know the appropriate repertoires of being a "good school student," that their failure to take them up is a matter of choice, and that they choose not to do them. On this reading, they simply have to learn, through the application of consequences, to choose to act within the range of acceptable behaviors. This humanist reading, which places all responsibility for correct action on individual students, is highly problematic. How students come to be read as taking up good behavior is not as simple as it might seem to teachers caught up in the discourses of schooling. What counts as "good behavior" is highly dependent on the teachers' beliefs about who the student "really is." It is our observation that if Shane had often displayed good student behaviors, *and if he had been recognized by staff as one who displayed them,* there is a good chance that his wearing of a hat in assembly would not have been read as bad behavior (Honan, Knobel, Baker, and Davies, forthcoming). It would have been assumed that *he had good reasons* for wearing a hat (i.e., that he was a rational human being), even though these reasons might not be immediately visible. Shane did later say what he should have done—simply taken off his hat as he was told and put up with the embarrassment. He also said he knew what the consequences of his actions would be as he was doing it—even before doing it. We suggest that the very act of telling him in front of the assembled students to take off his hat was an allocation of the subject position Shane was to occupy—that of an irrational student in need of the application of consequences.

It is worth commenting that even in the "rational" humanist discourse there is often no logical reason for the rules so fervently enforced. Perhaps teachers often realize the silliness of some of the rules they come to expect themselves to enforce, and a student's refusal to comply with them makes the ridiculousness of some rules all the more visible. For the child who is regarded as not behaving in ways informed by "reason," the major issue is about learning to conform, to be subjected, to become the rational humanist self who "chooses" correctly. When rules are a nonsense, the only purpose of the rule becomes for students to display their subjection, so teachers in their turn can *recognize* them as legitimate and well-adjusted students.

The power of positioning the students as *recognizably* able to engage in good student behaviors has been evident on many occasions in Cath's school. She talks about them and to them about the performance of themselves as "normal":

> We had a visit from a theatre group today. Shane was helping me get the room ready.
> *Shane:* Miss, aren't you worried about what we might do when we have these people here?
> *Cath:* Not at all, Shane. It's just like when we go out—I'm sure everyone will "do normal" while these people are here.
> And they all did—perfect behavior while they were there. (Cath's journal)

Contrary to the perceptions of the teachers in Shane's school, the students in Cath's school can be seen to invest a great deal of emotional energy in "getting it right," in becoming recognizable to themselves and to others as "students" (as properly subjected). The following entry from Cath's diary records Fred's valiant struggle to position himself as recognizably male:

> At camp, I was in the toilet and watched Fred walking across from the dam by himself. He's got no shoes on and is stepping on all these burrs. They must be hurting as he's crying. He starts saying to himself "stay cool, stay cool" and repeats this over and over until he finds a patch of dirt to sit on and pull them out. He's still got tears rolling down his face but saying his mantra. I walk out to the front door to see him coming around the corner—not a tear in sight and his typical swagger. (Cath's journal)

The so-called generalizability and context-free nature of the rational self is achieved at some cost. It leaves little room for personal idiosyncrasy (Walkerdine, 1988). Fred cannot ask for help and show others that he is hurt and at the same time accomplish a performance of himself in which he will be recognized as a proper male. To be a boy on such occasions is to suppress emotions—to do it all yourself and especially not to cry. To do so would not be getting it right as a boy. So he must fix it himself and not let the other boys see. The so-called natural practice of mastery of reason entails suppression of emotion, which Fred achieves on this occasion, and so he "gets it right" as a boy.

Notwithstanding Fred's moment of supreme control, Cath's students, who are categorized by the system as "disturbed," are seen to display behaviors that are assumed to arise from an excess of emotion and a lack of control of this excess. They can be violent and abusive to teachers and to other students. They are not able to act powerfully and get away with it, as did the "naughty boys" in the regular/mainstream school. While these boys recognizably perform the available repertoires of being "good school students" and "getting it right" as a boy, they do not produce these repertoires often enough for them to be recognizable as "good school students." Rather, their performances are generally read as unacceptable flaunting of power and violence (they have not "understood" that violence is only acceptable in some circumstances, such as on the football field). This reading is held together by the assumption that "understanding" and action are necessarily linked. Failure to engage in what is recognized as acceptable is not read as a failure to recognize on the part of the viewer, but as a disturbance "in" the child—a disturbance that needs correcting. Thus even when they do "good school student" they are not able to be recognized as such. The range of behaviors they engage in is too broad and too unpredictable for those in authority to see them as coherent, rational, *recognizable* selves. While some of that unpredictability and emotional display might be entirely "reasonable" behavior for someone finding themselves with no access to legitimate power, that is not usually an available reading for someone in authority over children.

Seeing the impact of humanist discourse

Cath's training to become principal of a special school for students positioned as emotionally disturbed/behavior disordered has involved major exposure to the dominant developmental/categorizing psychological discourses. These discourses provide a repertoire of ready-to-hand interpretations. An extract from Cath's journal shows how poststructuralist theory makes these discourses and the interpretive work they engender visible and revisable:

Bob is twelve and always "off" when the bigger kids—particularly George—come into the room. I went over today and he was running around being a real pain—but not really out of control.

Cath: Bob, why do you do this stuff when George and others are here?

Bob: Don't know but it's not why you think it is?

[I'm surprised that he thought I had a clue!]

Cath: What do you think I think the reason is?

Bob: You think that I'm scared when the others are here so I do this so I won't get hurt.

Cath: And it's not that?

Bob: No.

Cath: OK. Would you like to come and send some faxes for me?

Bob: OK.

Bob positions Cath as a helping professional—one who is able to talk through with him "why" he acts as he does. Cath is also taking up this discourse as she asks him "why?" But in her notes she articulates that she does not know "why" and questions the discourse that positions the adult as the expert—capable of pouring into the child the rationality that will change his behavior.

She reads Bob as knowing the developmental/categorizing psychological discourse at least as well as she does. He gives to her, and then is able to attribute to her, a very insightful explanation. In this discourse, if she had chosen to stay within it, she could have made an interesting power move and constituted Bob not as knowing the discourse and knowing how to use it competently, but as knowing nothing, as being, instead, in denial. It could be read as him knowing what the "real reason" is, but unable to say it for himself and so attributing it to Cath's knowing. Cath could have been flattered at Bob's attributing to her an insightful explanation of his behavior. At the same time, the insight he was denying would have been taken as a promising insight indicating an advance on his understanding of himself—a sign that he understands his behavior and that he will now be that one step closer to being able to change it. If this was the reading, Bob could have learned to see feelings and rationality at opposite ends of some continuum rather than rationality being merely a culturally privileged form of emotional experience (Hollway, 1989).

From a poststructuralist perspective, Cath can read Bob as both using and rejecting a particular psychological discourse. He rejects an explanation that produces him as weak, as flawed in the take-up of himself as "boy." (Bob routinely engages in excellent performances of masculinity that are recognized as such by the other boys.) At the same time, in this and other conversations, he uses psychological discourse in ways that keep him out of trouble—that demonstrate insight to Cath, giving her a sense of achievement as a caring female professional. Yet he denies this explanation—he recognizes it as an explanation and rejects it.

Cath could have been drawn into a debate about why he behaved as he did, and taken him up on his rejection of a perfectly plausible explanation. She could have drawn on the discourse of "denial," which would define him as saying "no" when he knows it is really a "yes." Bob would have been used to people knowingly hearing a "no" and looking as though they had heard a "yes." He may have been relieved that she accepted the "no" and did not look at him as though he was "in denial."

In spite of him offering her an explanation within a particular psychological discourse, she accepts his rejection of it and explores no further. This was difficult for her to do. She wanted to explore his explanation—to see if he was feeling safe—to talk about the things that he might need to do so that he could do the right thing in class. Instead, she positioned him as one who has the power to reject the constitutive force of demeaning discourses. In doing this she makes him recognizable as a legitimate student. If she had challenged his reading of himself she would have continued the cycle that has had Bob involved in "special" education for the "disturbed" for more than half of his school life. There is nothing to lose, and so much to gain, in taking the time to examine the discourses that hold student and principal in their places.

Bob did not send any faxes—he took his work and did it quietly, letting Cath get on with her work. No feedback or reinforcement. No "consequences." Just another place to do his work—be a student—away from some of the scenes in which violent others in his class were engaged. Cath and Bob collaborate to achieve a moment of resistance to the patterns in which he was caught up. Cath positioned Bob as one who had the right to speak and be heard. It would be reading too much into the situation to suggest that he had agency in the sense that he could articulate the multiple and contradictory ways in which he positions himself and is positioned in the various discourses he encounters, though it would be true to say that he powerfully used the discourses that shaped him for purposes other than those imagined by those who shaped him (Butler, 1997).

Davies (1992, p. 56) suggests "individuals who understand the processes through which they are made subject are better positioned to resist particular forms of subjectivity rather than cling to them through a mistaken belief that they are their own—that they signal who they are." In her analysis, Butler suggests how this might happen—how the subject is itself a site of ambivalence in which the subject emerges both as the *effect* of a prior power and as a *condition of possibility* for a radically conditioned form of agency (Butler, 1997, p. 14). The process of subordination may in itself provide the condition for the possibility of agency. As power subjugates, it may be that at some point a reversal and concealment occurs and power emerges as what belongs exclusively to the subject (making the subject appear as if it belonged to no prior operation of power). Power forms subjects, but subjects may come to believe that they own the power, that power is within them, and not see how power has operated to form them. Moreover, what is enacted by the subject is enabled but not finally contained by the prior working of power. The power that forms the subject may in that very formation be transformed—be different from the power that is/can be exercised by the subject. In exceeding the power by which it is enabled, agency becomes a possibility for the subject (Butler, 1997, p. 15). If the subject is *neither* fully determined by power *nor* fully determining of power—but significantly and partially both—Butler (p. 30) asks, "[I]s there a way to affirm complicity as the basis of political agency yet insist that political agency may do more than reiterate the conditions of subordination?" Is there a way that we can do more than acknowledge and come to understand the power that forms us and use that understanding to do something different both within and outside the confines of that forming power? Is agency possible in this way?

In the following episode, Cath reflexively examines the discourses through which she is constituting herself as principal and she abandons them in favor of another. In doing so she hands Robert a moment of being recognized as someone with agency. The effect on him and on Cath is electrifying:

Robert (an eleven-year-old) was on the roof today—calling out that he hates all of us—that he's going to burn the school down—that we're all stuffed. He's screaming about some injustice that happened to Paul (a younger boy with whom he travels to school).

He has not been to regular school for two years and I know that the police won't go around to his home without taking two cars. I wonder what I will do, as I know that if he really goes off he could do some damage.

Cath: Be careful up there, it can get slippery.

Robert: Get fucked. You're all bastards.

I have some choices about what to say next—to ask what happened, to enter negotiations, to talk about consequences and making good or bad choices about

behavior. Instead I tried to reflect on the discourse in which he is operating. To look at this rebel, wronged, positioned against the always right, in control teacher.
Cath: I didn't know this about you.
Robert: Fucking what?
Cath: I didn't know that you had such a strong sense of justice and will do just about anything if you thought a friend had been wronged.
  Silence. He comes down from the roof, picks up his bag, and goes to class. Later I went over to see what's happening and he was sitting down, just doing his work. (Cath's journal)

In this moment Robert the delinquent becomes Robert the protester—Robert the boy who has a right to be heard. We do not understand this as a change in the "essential Robert" but as a shift in positioning that may or may not be taken up by Robert (or made available to Robert) on future occasions.

Cath's repertoire of principal behaviors, drawn from the psychological/rational/educational/consequences discourse, seemed useless to Cath faced with this "out of control" student. As principal, she might have called his parents to come and get him—but the damage he could have done while waiting could have been extensive, and they have no phone. She might have gathered other staff to force him from the roof—further embedding both of them into patterns of power and powerlessness. She might have simply ignored him—but this would have raised issues of not being able to control the students and created the further injustice of being ignored.

But she does her principal thing first—her duty of care—and tells him to be careful. She reads him as knowing that this is what she must do and he lets her know this by his response.

Then she tries to understand the storyline in which he is operating. This switch actually makes him hearable as someone who is in protest about wrongs—a rebel with a cause. Such a reading is outside school discourse in which students cannot display what appears to teachers to be excessive power. A cynical reading of this interaction might be that Cath conned him down—fooled him. Our reading is that the shift Cath engaged in opened up a different space in which it was possible for her and for Robert to see that resistance to being a "good school student" is not necessarily mad or bad—but something that might matter in a positive sense and that can make him recognizable, by a person in authority, as someone to be valued.

We can assume that Robert already knew that being on the roof was not within the expected repertoire of school behaviors and that Cath did not have to tell him that. Neither did she have to tell him to go and do his school-work—she didn't and he did. Again, in this incident, Cath and Robert have collaborated in making it possible for Robert, and for Cath, to experience themselves as having agency, though of course we do not know what

Robert's experience was. What we do know is that, for this moment, they are not caught up in doing no more than "reiterating the conditions of subordination" (Butler, 1997, p. 30). Cath finds herself moving towards being able to see the processes through which she is made subject and is thus better positioned to resist particular forms of subjectivity, rather than cling to them through a mistaken belief that they are the truth about working with students. As he climbed down from the roof, perhaps even Robert was able to see the storylines that position him as "disturbed" and was able to take up the storyline of being in reasonable protest in some agentic way. If he did, his agency did not extend to being able to enter immediately into some negotiation about the problem with Paul. It could be that the unpracticed passage from out-of-control student to a recognizably worthy human being needs time to register, to take on board. And, of course, it is possible that he could not integrate it, finally, with the many other repeated moments of failure to be recognized as anything other than delinquent.

Being subjected can make available a power that rests on being recognizable and, in particular, being recognizable as legitimately taking oneself up in recognizable and laudable ways. The boys at Cath's school achieve being recognizable, but as "bad subjects" (which in Althusser's terms and within the psychological discourses means "not subjected"). But that is a structuralist reading. For Cath's students, the "good student" discourses have been imposed and have not been taken up in ways recognizable to the relevant authorities. A poststructuralist reading must take account of the psychic energy of the subjected being and what it is that they are doing with the imposed structures or discourses. These boys do perform themselves as subjected (Fred and the prickles, Bob and the psychological discourse, Robert getting down off the roof and working, the kids all "doing normal" when there are visitors at the school). They also perform acts of massive and heroic resistance (Robert shouting on the roof, Bob refusing the psychological discourses, Shane walking out of assembly). They marshal a lot of energy to refuse the forms of subjection made available to them, but the subject position "disturbed" is waiting there to catch up their rebellion as something that can only be recognized as a lack (lack of adequate subjection) by those in authority. By working in a poststructuralist framework, Cath is able, momentarily, to break the mold: she recognizes them as already subjected and as having the kind of power that comes from that subjection. As Butler (1997, p. 27) observes:

> [S]ubjection is the paradoxical effect of a regime of power in which the very "conditions for existence," the possibility of continuing as a recognizable social being, requires the formation and maintenance of the subject in subordination.

Butler (p. 28) asks, "[W]ithout a repetition that risks life—in its current organization—how might we begin to imagine the contingency of that organization, and performatively reconfigure the contours of the conditions of life?" In this chapter we have examined how it is possible to performatively reconfigure the contours. We have shown how discourses (including and especially particular psychological and educational discourses) are powerfully constitutive of the selves we take ourselves to be. We have shown how subjects who are read as not acting as if they are properly subjected are also read as the cause of their own "disordered behavior" through a faulty constitution of themselves as selves. We have shown how teachers are shaped to read and interpret behaviors within a set of discourses that rob students of power and thus the possibility of agency. And finally we have shown how the take-up of poststructuralist discourse enables a radical disruption of the taken-for-granted readings of educational practices, so opening up moments in which the participants can go beyond the conditions of their subjection.

At the beginning of this chapter we asked what might agency look like for the "behaviorally disturbed" students who are defined as somehow having escaped their subjection. We would conclude that the reading that makes them seem to have so escaped is a gross misreading. These students, like anyone else, are constituted (and constitute themselves) through the available discourses. We have not, here, provided an answer as to why these students do not "knuckle under" in the way the processes of schooling would suggest they should, other than to suggest that they are so consistently read as not having done so that it becomes increasingly difficult for them to achieve a reading of themselves as anything other than "bad subjects." At the same time, we have suggested that there are conflicting discourses for boys in school. Managing being a boy and being a student at the same time can verge on the impossible, particularly if access to legitimate forms of studenthood are consistently denied. We have also suggested that the excessive deprivation of a sense of powerfulness could in itself serve as a partial explanation of the emotional excesses that these boys sometimes engage in.

~ Epilogue: On mor(t)ality

mortal: 1. (of living beings, esp. human beings) subject to death. 2. of or involving life or the world

morale: the degree of mental or moral confidence of a person or group; spirit of optimism

moral: concerned with or relating to human behaviour, esp. the distinction between good and bad or right and wrong behaviour . . .

—*Collins Dictionary of the English Language*

FOR THE LAST DECADE OF MY LIFE, as this body of writing demonstrates, I have been engaged in poststructuralist writing—in exploring the possibilities of making sense of the world against the grain of "common sense." This does not mean abandoning common sense, necessarily, but rather it means engaging in a dual motion of extracting myself from the weighty inevitability of common knowledges, and of finding creative and unexpected ways of knowing, of making sense. Poststructuralist theory shares some of the strategies of good political cartoonists and commentators, whose unexpected representations generate both a different way of looking and occasionally a refreshing burst of energy expressed in laughter. For me, poststructuralist theory has a wonderful capacity to generate energy and to open up freedoms as it unchains me from inevitabilities I might otherwise not be able to see, let alone find my way out of. One of those old inevitabilities is the humanist self. Instead of focusing only on continuities and predictabilities of self, poststructuralist theories of subjection also make visible the shifting relations of power, and the multiple, fragmented, sometimes contradictory processes of being/acting in the world.

From a poststructuralist perspective, we are subjected to powers that act on us, not only shaping or forming us in particular (and ongoing) ways, but more important, and at the same time and through the same processes, these powers provide the *conditions of our possibility* (Butler, 1997, p. 14). The humanist subject, in contrast, is coerced by forces that are conceptualized, in humanist discourses, as external to it. This subject who is coerced is, nevertheless, understood as a prediscursive or discourse-independent subject. The conditions of its possibility are internal to it. The humanist self, the "true" and "essential" self, must be forged out of itself. That self will then make "free" choices among a range of already existing ways of being. But the catch is that each choice will signal who the real (prechoice) person is. While it is understood that the individual will be subjected to enormous pressures from outside (peer pressure, the force of the law, and so on), s/he must be able to stand against any of these pressures or forces if s/he judges them to be wrong. The undisclosed trick that the humanist self has to achieve is to simultaneously be shaped, to lock into a commitment to retaining and remaining that shaped, rational, predictable self who makes sense within the terms of dominant discourses, and at the same time to make choices that arise from and signal who s/he *really is* independent of discourse and relations of power. An impossible task really, though one that many of us more or less accomplish—or go on attempting to accomplish. And that takes a lot of energy. It is enormously liberating to be freed from the attempt.

I notice this freedom most when others attempt to halt my feminist work by implying that what I am saying comes from an essential (and limited/faulty) self, rather than addressing the issue that I wish to be taken seriously. This conversational strategy includes statements such as "so you're just a liberal feminist" (when I am arguing that girls or women should not be denied access to opportunities on the basis of their sex/gender) or "you are oversensitive and make yourself unhappy unnecessarily by seeing offense where none is intended" (when I am drawing attention to patterns of language use that demean women and serve to hold them in powerless positions). I am able to reply to such assertions that the issue is not what "I am," but the discourses and practices through which oppressive social patterns are held in place. Seeing poststructurally makes visible both the systemic practices and the moment-by-moment work through which relations of power and powerlessness are played out. For me, this tends to increase the will to act, and the capacity to act, since it becomes possible to see the multiple and complex discourses and practices through which any particular situation is being put in place and held in place. It is also possible to see when there is inadequate information or analyses that might form a basis for action.

Yet many people fret about the abandonment of the essential humanist self and fulminate against poststructuralist writers for what they presume they will find in place of the abandoned humanist self—an immoral and unlawful being. Many of the authors in Parker (1998), for example, gathered all "relativists" together in one bundle, not even feeling the need to name them, and claimed them incapable of action or commitment. And certainly it is so, that when I am thinking poststructurally, I am less given to blind obedience to the rules or sentiments that others might wish to be taken up, universally, as always and inevitably "right." Thinking poststructurally makes me very nervous about such universal claims as the basis for action.

Reflecting on the implications of acting in one way or another, or adopting one discourse or another, shifts in subtle ways when one thinks in terms of some of the possibilities opened up in poststructuralist thought. Since no moral discourse has absolute status, then in relation to any "ought" statement, questions have to be asked, such as: Who is the author of this statement? Where does his or her authority lie? And what are the effects in this particular situation, and at this particular point in time and with these people involved, of taking up the terms of this statement? And perhaps more important, what is hidden by this statement? And what competing discourses are at play? These questions are not asked destructively, but deconstructively, the point being to understand the statement differently—in a sense, against the grain of itself. Moral action is not taken up because it comes from someone with authority, or because it has popular support, but because it can be mobilized effectively in a particular situation to bring about, for example, a particular desired set of interactive practices, or to shift awareness in some way that the speaker, or group of speakers, have decided is important, life-giving—yet all the while recognizing the provisional and temporary nature of the answers it is possible to provide to any of the questions asked.

And of course, deciding what is important is also not automatic and can never provide any more than a provisional basis for action. One asks of any claim to importance, important to whom? And why? What values are at play when importance is given in that way? What other values are cast aside or hidden by such a position? What else that might be important is obscured if this becomes the basis for action? Such questions have become increasingly useful to me in my everyday work life in attempting to understand the discourses and practices of new managerialism, which are anything but life-giving, sapping the morale of workers and denuding people of their humanity. New managerialism has been taken up almost without question in my own university. Its clever use of economic rationalist discourses accompanied by "value" words like "quality" and "effectiveness" combined with pressures from government for its adoption make it hard to resist. I find it deeply distressing to see the disappearance of principled decision making on the part of managers, as their sole focus becomes more effective exploitation of the increasingly demoralized workers. The press of new managerialism, when I was in a management position, was visible and repugnant to me. Its adoption made everyone who worked within its terms less human.

"But isn't this constant questioning and resistance very tiring?" you might ask, and "How can you be sure that you are right?" To the first question I would answer no, I find it exhilarating more often than I find it exhausting, and the exhaustion is not nearly so debilitating as not being able to see how and through what discourses and practices I am being constituted and positioned. And to the second question I would answer that although I cannot know I am right in any universalistic sense, I nevertheless feel myself on mor(t)al ground, a ground on which questions about the meaning of "humanity," and of what it means to be human, are opened up rather than closed down with unquestionable and authoritative answers.

In abandoning the automatic connection between ways of speaking and an essential self, and in heightening the awareness of the different discourses and relations of power at play and their effects, I find a different mor(t)ality. I am no longer tied down by questions as to whether my actions constitute one coherent package called the "real me." The emphasis shifts away from "Is this how *I* would speak or act?" to "If I speak or act this way, *what emerges* in that speaking and acting?" And as I watch/listen/smell/feel the emergent speaking or acting, I can see what is emerging not just as the effect of my acting or speaking in a particular way, but also as a new moment in which the context, the lived history of the participants and their understanding of the present moment, will all be constitutive of my speech, my action. Reflection moves away from self and towards action. And action moves away from repeated practices to movement between possible practices, and more important, towards different ways of understanding practice and its implications. This does not mean that obsessing about "self" ceases, or that fixed patterns do not occasionally get lodged, apparently intractably—but that the possibility of this reorientation is there.

Inevitably, from time to time I find myself immersed in a discourse that I am not aware of at the time, or find myself unable to pick apart the various discourses and relations of power that are at play in a particular space/time. I may catch myself being carried along by the force of a discourse that I do not, at that point in time, have the skill or resources to question. I am swept up, along with others, in ways of seeing and being that escape my reflexive gaze. And when I do manage to catch myself in the act of being constituted (and constitutive), what it is that poststructuralist analytic strategies will enable me to see in that particular space/time cannot be predicted or guaranteed. It is, on the contrary, the multiplication of possible ways of seeing and being that is poststructuralism's special charm—and power.

The repeated claim that poststructuralist theory is immoral because it does not accept the claim that there must be a set of absolute moral values seems to me to be no more than part of a word game. It is an extension of the powerful word game in which absolute values are established by those who have an investment in locking others into controllable patterns, patterns that are of benefit to those originating the game. The claim that poststructuralists (and others like them) are immoral and incapable of action has little to do with what I experience of lived reality as it unfolds moment by moment and in particular contexts. And it has little to do with the way we each live our lives, tangled in a knotted web of discourses and passions, a web that is of our own making, and out of the substance of which we are continually being made up. We are both the weaver and the web. And that web is not one in/through which we are simply determined (though we are that), nor is it fixed. It is a web in which we can come to see the knots (our discursive practices, our ways of knowing, our selving, our embeddedness in relations of power), and we can also come to see how to untie some of the knots or tie up different ones—or to actually spin/become new threads.

But because we are not humanist agents with absolute power over discourse, we also, inevitably, find old knots tied back up in our own practices or in the practices of others, and the fabric we are weaving has its own never-finished, surprising, and sometimes frustrating life. As Hillevi Lenz-Taguchi wrote to me on reading an earlier draft of this epilogue:

> Feelings of transgression give me a temporary feeling of freedom, which fades away. In the very process of persistent weaving, I am always in a state of resistance, where knots untied will stick up their grinning faces again and again, and where I as a weaving subject will always struggle with being meshed within the fabric—wanting it badly and hating it! But simultaneously—with joy, fear and pain—I spin those delicate threads that necessarily "go against the grain," making the fabric uneven or leaving it with mysterious holes of uncertainties, doubts, desires and excitements.

A poststructuralist approach does not *guarantee* good action and good outcomes. But neither does it block them. And discourses that provide such guarantees are not, and probably never have been, exempt from generating pain and suffering. What poststructuralist theorizing does is open up discourses and practices to questioning, and provide strategies for questioning, that run against the grain of common sense and of dominant (and dominating) discourses and practices.

Foucault (in Rabinow, 1994, p. 144), for example, when asked whether homosexuals should be allowed to teach in schools, since they might corrupt school children if allowed to teach them, replied:

> The whole question, you see, has been wrongly formulated. Under no circumstances should the sexual choice of an individual determine the profession he is allowed, or forbidden, to practice. Sexual practices simply fall outside the pertinent factors related to the suitability for a given profession. "Yes," you might say, "but what if the profession is used by homosexuals to encourage others to become homosexual?"
>
> Well let me ask you this: Do you believe that teachers who for years, for decades, for centuries, explained to children that homosexuality is intolerable; do you believe that the textbooks that purged literature and falsified history in order to exclude various types of sexual behaviour, have not caused ravages at least as serious as a homosexual teacher who speaks about

homosexuality and who can do no more harm than explain a given reality, a lived experience?

Foucault (pp. 147–48) goes on after this example to reiterate the importance of the possibility of movement beyond what already exists:

> [T]he important question here, it seems to me, is not whether a culture without restraints is possible or even desirable but whether the system of constraints in which a society functions leaves individuals the liberty to transform the system. Obviously constraints of any kind are going to be intolerable to certain segments of society. The necrophiliac finds it intolerable that graves are not accessible to him. But a system of constraints becomes truly intolerable when the individuals who are affected by it don't have the means of modifying it.

Poststructuralist theory does give greater mor(t)al responsibility to the subjects who use it, simply because they cannot rely on the certainties that others have put in place, and so involves an acute awareness of life, and of being in and of the world. Poststructuralist theory invites an openness to the unexpected, it turns a critical gaze towards oppressive patterns of power and powerlessness, and it engages a strong will to action. Further, Derrida (1992, p. 83) says, that for him, deconstructive work does not proceed without love:

> Deconstruction as such is reducible to neither a method nor an analysis (the reduction to simple elements); it goes beyond critical decision itself. That is why it is not negative, even though it has often been interpreted as such despite all sorts of warnings. For me it always accompanies an affirmative exigency, I would even say that it never proceeds without love. . . .

Deconstruction, for me, has meant a turning away of the reflexive gaze from the achievement and maintenance of an essential self and towards the folding and unfolding of life's possibilities. The success of life cannot be judged on how well I fit my allotted categories ("Am I a good woman?") or on how well I position myself within dominant discourses ("What prizes and recognition have I had?"). Instead, the categories through which we are each positioned, the processes of positioning, and the discursive practices through which such positioning is made possible and defensible are made both visible and revisable. From a poststructuralist perspective, protests can be made against a particular mode of categorization, or against a positioning as powerless or subordinate, or against particular discourses. But these protests do not need to be made from the position of victim, or by attempting to insert oneself and pass within the terms of those who are positioned as powerful within dominant discourses, or by struggling to get a counter discourse up and running as "politically correct." Nor do they need to be made by aligning oneself with a particular "correct" discourse. Instead, it is possible to analyze the complex interplay of multiple overlapping discourses and of positions of power and powerlessness as people vie for the world they desire, or believe in, to be brought into being. Each of the conflicting discourses can be deconstructed, and on the basis of seeing the detail of each at work, lines of preferred action can be worked out.

Finally, as a researcher/analyst/critic, what I love about poststructuralist theory is the chance to tease out the fine detail of how a discourse works, to find its subtleties and its lack of subtlety, to find how not to be blinded by existing categories and definitions, but to listen, and to look, to feel, and to question, to turn inward and reflect, to make sense against the grain of common sense, and to find the aha! that allows the completely unexpected detail to be noticed, the shift in understanding to occur. Cixous provides many such moments. She speaks what was unspeakable until the moment she utters it. Using her own body, her own lived experience, as a resource, she finds the detail in something as apparently simple as a telephone conversation between lovers (like Derrida, she does not shrink from talk of love):

> [W]e will never be able to imagine love without the telephone. What did we do 'before' to make the most exquisite, the most intimate, the most delicate love, the most delicately loving? Love always needs telephones: this passage of the most naked voice, the most real and sublime voice directly to the ear of the heart, without transition, the voice never dares to be so naked as on the telephone. What I cannot say to you in the full light of presence I can say to you in the common night of the telephone. (Cixous, in Cixous and Calle-Gruber, 1997, p. 48)

Her awareness of language, in the power of its detail, is not limited to an examination of already existing language forms. She sees it as part of her work to invent new terms to express what she finds when she looks differently. "The ear of the heart" is much more than a poetic metaphor that allows us to attend to the detail of how conversations between lovers might be experienced. It is also a way of imagining the embodied being against the grain of the mind/body binary—in which the brain is the only bit of the body caught up in knowing, with the rest of the body relegated to an inferior slave-like subordinate status. Such writing expands our capacity as readers to recognize the detailed texts of our selving, and at the same time it increases the possibilities of selving—of recognizing the unfolding multiple self as being much more than already existing discourses made possible. This release from the narrow "oughts" of writing and of academic thought generates, in my experience, a sense of freedom and energy and at the same time draws my attention to the enormous power of words. I have come to understand, through reading Cixous, that my real work is done in the act of writing. The book I wrote at the same time as I was putting this collection together, *(In)scribing Body/Landscape Relations*, seeks to write the body back into the landscapes from which it thought itself separate.

Roland Barthes, too, writes about love. In an interview about his book *A Lover's Discourse* (1978), the interviewer asks about the danger of writing/talking about "love," suggesting that not only is it out of fashion but it is not really a suitable topic for someone recently elected to the *Collège de France*. He then tries to catch Barthes up in an admission that the book is really autobiographical:

> *So then the lover who speaks is really you, Roland Barthes?*
>
> My answer may seem to be a pirouette, but it is not. The subject that I am is not unified. This is something I feel profoundly. To then say "It's I!" would be to postulate a unity of self that I do not recognize in myself.
>
> > *Allow me to rephrase my question: For each figure in the book, one after the other, do you say: "There I am"?*
>
> Well! ... When I conducted a research seminar on this same topic, I took into account figures that I had not experienced myself, figures taken from books. . . . But, obviously, that's what was cut from my book. Yes, I definitely have a personal relation to all the figures in the book. . . .
>
> . . . My book implies certain values.
>
> > *And a moral?*
>
> Yes, there is a moral.
>
> > *And that would be?*
>
> A morality of affirmation. One should not let oneself be swayed by disparagements of the sentiment of love. One should affirm. One should dare. Dare to love. . . . (Barthes, 1985, p. 305)

There are, in this example, several refreshing features, which go to the heart of poststructuralist thinking. Barthes does not fall into the interviewer's trap of revealing at last the "real Barthes." At the same time, he reveals a willingness to enter into disparaged topics, to take up positions within them, to dare to feel passionately and to make himself vulnerable by not proceeding in an orderly, controlled way. He began, he says, with a broad array of "figures" drawn from the literature, but in choosing what stayed in his book, he finds, on reflection, that it was what he had a personal relation to that he kept. Because the task of fitting the statement of "what is" into a preconceived "ought" is abandoned, the statement of what is must attend very carefully to its detailed unfolding. His honesty, here, works on at least two levels. It has led to a book in which we find not received wisdoms about love but a series of moments in which we are given permission to see what is there in ways we could not see before. The second kind of honesty is that the book was not written "objectively," but in relation to his own immersion in multiple and complex experiences of love. A difficult admission, but one that gives permission to others to look at the detail of their own writing and its connectedness to the usually invisible (or hidden) detail of their lived experiences. I find in this honesty, and in the openness to seeing beyond what is given, a capacity to attend much more carefully to human experience with all its grinning knots, and gaps, and passions.

I conclude this epilogue on mor(t)ality with words from Cixous (in Cixous and Calle-Gruber, 1997, p. 32):

When I say 'more human', I mean: progressing. I ought to say: better human. This means, while being human, not depriving oneself of the rest of the universe. It is to be able to echo—a complex but magnificent labour—with what constitutes the universe. . . . [W]e are not without an environment, one that is human, personalized, personal; and terrestrial, urban, etc. ('political' comes afterwards for me). We are all haunted by the question of our mortality. And thus haunted by the question of what it is to be human, this thing that speaks, that thinks, that loves, that desires and that one day is extinguished.

~ References

Althusser, L. (1971). *Lenin and philosophy and other essays.* London: New Left Books.

―――― (1984). *Essays on ideology.* London: New Left Books.

Bakhtin, M. M. (1981). *Discourse in the novel.* In M. Holquist (Ed.), The Dialogical Imagination. Austin: University of Texas Press.

Barthes, R. (1977). *A Lover's Discourse. Fragments.* (R. Howard, trans.). London: Penguin.

―――― (1984). *Camera lucida: Reflection on photography.* London: Flamingo.

―――― (1985). *The Grain of the Voice. Interviews 1962–1980.* Trans. L. Coverdale. Berkeley: University of California Press.

Benhabib, S. (1987). The generalised and the concrete other: The Kohlberg-Gilligan controversy and feminist theory. In E. F. Kittay and D. T. Meyers (Eds.), *Women and moral theory.* New Jersey: Rowman and Littlefield.

Benson, P. (1990). Feminist second thoughts about free agency. *Hypatia,* 5(3), 47–64.

Brooks, P. (1984). *Reading for the plot: Design and intention in narrative.* New York: Random House.

Brownstein, R. (1984). *Becoming a heroine: Reading about women in novels.* Harmondsworth, Australia: Penguin.

Burman, E. (1994). *Deconstructing developmental psychology.* New York: Routledge Kegan Paul.

Butler, J. (1990). *Gender trouble: Feminism and the subversion of identity.* New York: Routledge.

―――― (1992). Contingent foundations. In J. Butler and J. W. Scott (Eds.), *Feminists theorize the political.* New York: Routledge.

―――― (1993). *Bodies that matter: On the discursive limits of "sex."* New York: Routledge.

―――― (1995). Contingent foundations: Feminism and the question of "postmodernism." In S. Benhabib, J. Butler, D. Cornell, and N. Fraser (Eds.), *Feminist contentions: A philosophical exchange.* New York: Routledge.

―――― (1997). *The psychic life of power.* Stanford, CA: Stanford University Press.

Carbaugh, D. (1988/89). Deep agony: "Self vs society" in Donahue discourse. *Research on Language and Social Interaction* 22, 179–212.

Cixous, H. (1981). The laugh of the medusa. In E. Marks and I. de Courtivron (Eds.), *New French feminisms: An anthology.* Brighton, UK: The Harvester Press.

―――― (1986). Sorties: Out and out: Attacks/ways out/forays. In H. Cixous and C. Clément (Eds.), *The newly born woman.* Manchester: Manchester University Press.

Cixous, H. and M. Calle-Gruber (1997). *Hélène Cixous rootprints: Memory and life writing* (E. Prenowitz, Trans.). London: Routledge.

—— (1986). *The newly born woman.* Manchester: Manchester University Press.

Clément, C. (1986). The guilty one. In H. Cixous and C. Clément (Eds.), *The newly born woman.* Manchester: Manchester University Press.

Clément, H. (1988). *Opera, or the undoing of women* (B. Wing, Trans.). Minneapolis: University of Minnesota Press.

Cohen, P. and M. Somerville (1990). *Ingelba and the five black matriarchs.* Sydney: Allen and Unwin.

Connell, R. W. (1987). *Gender and power.* Sydney: Allen and Unwin.

Coppierters, F. (1981). *Social psychology and improvised theatre.* University of Antwerp Doctoral dissertation.

Corsaro, W. (1979). We're friends right?: Children's use of access rituals in a nursery school. *Language in Society* 8, 315–36.

Couzens Hoy, D. (1986). Power, repression, progress: Foucault, Lukes, and the Frankfurt School. In D. Couzens Hoy (Ed.), *Foucault: A critical reader.* Oxford: Blackwell.

Crane, D. (1995). A personal postscript, an impostured preface. In J. Gallop (Ed.), *Pedagogy: The question of impersonation.* Bloomington: Indiana University Press.

Cunningham, G. (1989). Called into existence: Desire, gender and voice in Frederick Douglass's narrative of 1845. *Differences: A Journal of Feminist Cultural Studies* 1(Fall), 108–136.

Davies, B. (1982). *Life in the classroom and playground: The accounts of primary school children.* London: Routledge and Kegan Paul.

—— (1983). The role pupils play in the social construction of classroom order. *British Journal of Sociology of Education* 4(1), 55–69.

—— (1989a). *Frogs and snails and feminist tales: Preschool children and gender.* Sydney: Allen and Unwin.

—— (1989b). The discursive production of the male/female dualism in school settings. *Oxford Review of Education* 15(3), 229–41.

—— (1989c). Life sentences. In D. Brown, H. Ellyard, and B. Polkinhorne (Eds.), *Angry women: An anthology of Australian women's writing.* Sydney: Hale and Iremonger.

—— (1990). The problem of desire. *Social Problems* 37(4), 501–516.

—— (1991). The concept of agency: A feminist poststructuralist analysis. *Social Analysis* 30, 42–53.

—— (1992). Women's subjectivity and feminist stories. In C. Ellis and M. Flaherty (Eds.), *Investigating subjectivity: Research on lived experience.* Newbury Park, CA: Sage.

—— (1993). *Shards of glass: Children reading and writing beyond gendered identities.* Sydney: Allen and Unwin.

—— (1994). *Poststructuralist theory and classroom practice.* Geelong, Australia: Deakin University Press.

—— (1996a). *Power/knowledge/desire: Changing school organisation and management practices.* Canberra: Department of Education, Employment and Youth Affairs.

—— (1996b). What makes Australian education strange: Australian education in the Asian context. In *Australia in its Asian Context, Occasional Paper Series 1/1996.* Canberra: Academy of the Social Sciences in Australia.

—— (1997). The subject of poststructuralism: A reply to Alison Jones. *Gender and Education* 9(3), 271–83.

—— (1998). Psychology's subject: A commentary on the relativism/realism debate. In I. Parker (Ed.), *Social constructionism, discourse and realism.* London: Sage.

—— (2000). *(In)scribing Body/landscape Relations.* Walnut Creek, CA: AltaMira Press.

Davies, B., S. Dormer, E. Honan, N. McAllister, R. O'Reilly, S. Rocco, and A.Walker (1997). Ruptures in the skin of silence: A collective biography. *Hecate* 23(1), 62–79.

Davies, B. and R. Harré (1990). Positioning: The discursive production of selves. *Journal for the Theory of Social Behavior* 20(1), 43–63.

Davies, B. and R. Hunt (1994) Classroom competencies and marginal positioning. *British Journal of Sociological Education* 15(3), 389–408.

Davies, B. and C. Laws (1999) Poststructuralist theory in practice: Working with "behaviorally disturbed" children. *International Journal for Qualitative Studies in Education*

Davies, B. and K. Munro (1987). The perception of order in apparent disorder: A classroom scene observed. *Journal of Education for Teaching* 13(2), 117–31.

de Beauvoir, S. (1972). *The second sex.* Harmondsworth: Penguin.

de Lauretis, T. (1987). *Technologies of gender: Essays in theory, film and fiction.* Bloomington: Indiana University Press.

Deleuze, G. (1992). Ethology, Spinoza and us. In J. Crary and S. Kwinter (Eds.), *Incorporations.* New York: Zone.

—— (1995). *Negotiations 1972–1990* (M. Joughlin, Trans.). New York: Columbia University Press.

Deleuze, G. and F. Guattari (1987). *A thousand plateaus: Capitalism and schizophrenia* (R. Massumi, Trans.). Minneapolis: University of Minnesota Press.

Deleuze, G. and C. Parnet (1987). *Dialogues* (H. Tomlinson and B. Habberjam, Trans.). London: Athlone.

Derrida, J. (1992). *Points . . . Interviews 1974–994.* (E. Weber, ed. P. Kamuf and others, trans.). Stanford, CA: Stanford University Press.

Edgar, E. (1998). Where does the weather come from? A response to Behavioral Disorders: A postmodern perspective. *Behavioral Disorders* 23(3), 160–65.

Edwards, A. (1983). Sex roles: A problem for the sociology of women. *The Australian and New Zealand Journal of Sociology* 19(3), 385–412.

Elkind, D. (1998). Behavioral disorders: A postmodern perspective. *Behavioral Disorders* 23(3), 153–59.

Farmer, B. (1990). *A body of water.* St Lucia: University of Queensland Press.

Flax, J. (1993). *Disputed subjects: Essays on psychoanalysis, politics and philosophy.* New York: Routledge.

Foucault, M. (1977). What is an author. In D. Bouchard (Ed.), *Language, Counter-memory, Practice.* Ithaca, NY: Cornell University Press.

—— (1980). *The history of sexuality (Vol. 1).* New York: Vintage.

—— (1983). The subject and power. In H. Dreyfus and P. Rabinow (Eds.), *Michel Foucault: Beyond structuralism and hermeneutics.* Chicago: University of Chicago Press.

—— (1984). Nietzsche, genealogy and history. In P. Rabinow, (Ed.), *The Foucault reader.* Harmondsworth: Penguin.

—— (1988). Technologies of the self. In L. H. Martin, H. Gutman, and P. H. Hutton (Eds.), *Technologies of the Self.* Amherst: The University of Massachusetts Press.

Frazer, L. (1990). Feminist talk and talking about feminism. *Oxford Review of Education* 15(3), 281–90.

Friedan, B. (1963). *The feminine mystique.* Harmondsworth: Penguin.

Frye, M. (1990). A response to Lesbian ethics. *Hypatia* 5(3), 133–37.

Fuery, P. (1995). *Theories of desire.* Melbourne: Melbourne University Press.

Goffman, E. (1974). *Frame analysis.* New York: Harper and Row.

—— (1981). *Forms of talk.* Oxford: Blackwell.

Gramsci, A. (1957). *The modern prince and other writings.* New York: International.

Grosz, E. (1989). *Sexual subversions.* Sydney: Allen and Unwin.

—— (1990). Inscriptions and body-maps: Representation and the corporeal. In T. Threadgold and A. Cranny-Francis (Eds.), *Feminine masculine and representation.* Sydney: Allen and Unwin.

Haraway, D. (1988). Situated knowledges: The science question in feminism and the privilege of partial perspective. *Feminist Studies* 14(3), 575–99.

Harré, R. (1979). *Social being.* Totawa, NJ: Rowman and Littlefield.

—— (1983). *Personal being.* Cambridge, MA: Harvard University Press.

Harré, R. and P. F. Secord (1973). *The explanation of social behavior.* Oxford: Blackwell.

Harris, R. (1982). *The language makers.* London: Duckworth.

Haug, F., et al. (1987). *Female sexualisation.* London: Verso.

Hazel, V. (1996). *The politics of voice.* Australian Feminist Studies 11(24), 309–16.

Henriques, J., W. Hollway, C. Urwin, C. Venn, and V. Walkerdine (Eds.) (1984). *Changing the subject: Psychology, social regulation and subjectivity.* London: Methuen.

Hite, M. (1989). *The other side of the story: Structures and strategies of contemporary feminist narratives.* Ithaca, NY: Cornell University Press.

Hollway, W. (1984). Gender difference and the production of subjectivity. In J. Henriques, W. Hollway, C. Urwin, C. Venn, and V. Walkerdine (Eds.),

Changing the subject: Psychology, social regulation and subjectivity. London: Methuen.

——— (1989). *Subjectivity and method in psychology.* London: Sage.

Honan, E., M. Knobel, C. Baker and B. Davies, (forthcoming). The accomplishment of good studenthood: Multiple readings. *Qualitative Inquiry.*

Irigaray, L. (1985). *This sex which is not one.* Ithaca, NY: Cornell University Press.

Jones, A. (1997). Teaching poststructuralist feminist theory in education: Student resistances. *Gender and Education* 9(3), 262–69.

Kamler, B., R. Maclean, J. Reid, and A. Simpson (1993). *Shaping up nicely: The formation of schoolgirls and schoolboys in the first month of school.* A Report to the Gender Equity and Curriculum Reform Project, Geelong: Department of Employment, Education and Training with Deakin University.

Kantor, R. (1988). Creating school meaning in preschool curriculum. *Theory into Practice* 27(1), 25–35.

Kauffman, J. M. (Ed.) (1998a). *Behavioral Disorders* 23(3).

——— (1998b). Are we all postmodernists now? *Behavioral Disorders* 23(3), 149–52.

Kearney, R. (1994). Jacques Derrida. In R. Kearney (Ed.), *Dialogues with contemporary continental philosophers: The phenomenological heritage.* Manchester: Manchester University Press.

Keillor, G. (1986). *Lake Wobegon days.* New York: Penguin.

Kessler, S. J., and W. McKenna (1978). *Gender: An ethnomethodological approach.* Chicago: University of Chicago Press.

Kristeva, J. (1986 [1981]). Women's time. In T. Moi (Ed.), *The Kristeva reader.* Oxford: Blackwell.

Lacan, J. (1966). *Ecrits.* London: Tavistock.

Le Guin, U. (1983). *Left hand of darkness.* New York: Ace Books.

Levine, M. (1991). Translator's introduction. In S. Weber (Ed.), *Return to Freud.* Jacques Lacan's dislocation of psychoanalysis. Cambridge: Cambridge University Press.

Lugones, M. (1990). Hispaneando y lesbiando: On Sarah Hoagland's lesbian ethics. *Hypatia* 5(3), 139–46.

McDermott, R. P. (1976). *Kids make sense: An ethnographic account of the interactional management of success and failure in one first-grade classroom.* Unpublished doctoral dissertation, Stanford University.

McNay, L. (1992) *Foucault and feminism: Power, gender and the self.* Cambridge: Polity Press.

——— (1994). *Foucault: A critical introduction.* Cambridge: Polity Press.

Mellor, B. and A. Patterson (1996). Reading capacities: Foundations or formulae? *Interpretations* 29(3), 46–69.

Moi, T. (1987). *Sexual textual politics: Feminist literary theory.* London: Methuen.

——— (1989). Feminist literary criticism. In A. Jefferson and D. Robey (Eds.), *Modern literary theory.* London: B. T. Batsford Ltd.

Muhlhausler, P. and R. Harré (1990). *Pronouns and people.* Oxford: Blackwell.

Munsch, R. (1980). *The paperbag princess.* Toronto: Annick Press.

Nye, A. (1989). The voice of the serpent? French feminism and philosophy of language. In A. Garry and M. Pearsail (Eds.), *Women, knowledge and reality.* Boston: Unwin Hyman.

Parker, I. (1989). *The crisis in modern social psychology—and how to end it.* London: Routledge and Kegan Paul.

——— (Ed.) (1998). *Social constructionism, discourse and realism.* London: Sage.

Pearce, W. B. (1989). *Communication and the human condition.* Cardondale, IL: Southern Illinois University Press.

Pearce, W. B. and V. Cronen (1981). *Communication, action and meaning.* New York: Praeger.

Porter, E. (1991). *Women and moral identity.* Sydney: Allen and Unwin.

Potter, J. and M. Wetherall (1988). *Social psychology and discourse.* London: Routledge.

Rabinow, P. (ed) (1997). *Michel Foucault. Ethics, subjectivity and truth.* (R. Hurley and others, trans.). New York: The New Press.

Ricouer, P. (1979). The model of the text: Meaningful action considered as text. In P. Rabinow and W. Sullivan (Eds.), *Interpretive social science: A reader.* Berkeley: University of California Press.

Riviere, J. (1986). Womanliness as a masquerade. In V. Burgin, J. Donald, and C. Kaplan (Eds.), *Formations of fantasy.* London: Methuen.

Rogers, L. (1988). Biology, the popular weapon: Sex differences in cognitive function. In B. Caine, E. Grosz, and M. de Lervanche (Eds.), *Crossing boundaries: Feminisms and the critique of knowledges.* Sydney: Allen and Unwin.

Rose, N. (1985). *The psychological complex: Psychology, politics and society in England 1869–1939.* London: Routledge and Kegan Paul.

Ryan, M. (1989). *Politics and culture: Working hypotheses for a revolutionary society.* London: Macmillan.

Sayers, J. (1986). *Sexual contradictions: Psychology, psychoanalysis and feminism.* London: Tavistock.

Scheflen, A. E. (1973). *Communicational structure.* Bloomington: Indiana University Press.

Seidler, V. (1989). *Rediscovering masculinity: Reason, language and sexuality.* London: Routledge.

Smith, D. (1987). *The everyday world as problematic: A feminist sociology.* Boston: Northeastern University Press.

Smith, P. (1988). *Discerning the subject.* Minneapolis: University of Minnesota Press.

Søndergaard, D. M. (1999) Destabilising discourse analysis. Approaches to poststructuralist empirical research. In I. Henningsen (Ed.), *Kon i deu Akacemiske Organisation Working Paper Series no. 7.*

Stanley, L. and S. Wise (1983). *Breaking out: Feminist consciousness and feminist research.* London: Routledge and Kegan Paul.

Taylor, H. (1990). *So what about it Mr Menzies? Women's claims for citizenship, 1939–1941.* Paper presented at the "Woman/Australia/Theory Conference," Brisbane, July, 1990.

Trinh, M. (1989). *Woman, native, other: Writing, postcoloniality and feminism.* Bloomington: Indiana University Press.

Walkerdine, V. (1981). Sex, power and pedagogy. *Screen Education* 38, 14–24.

—— (1985). On the regulation of speaking and silence. In C. Steedman, C. Urwin, and V. Walkerdine (Eds.), *Language, gender and childhood.* London: Routledge and Kegan Paul.

—— (1987). Some day my prince will come. In A. McRobbie and M. Nava (Eds.), *Gender and generation.* London: Macmillan.

—— (1988). *The mastery of reason: Cognitive development and the production of rationality.* London: Routledge.

—— (1989). Femininity as performance. *Oxford Review of Education* 15(3), 267–79.

—— (1990). *Schoolgirl fictions.* London: Verso.

Walkerdine, V. and H. Lucey (1989). *Democracy in the kitchen: The regulation of mothers and the socialisation of daughters.* London: Virago.

Weber, S. (1991). *Return to Freud. Jacques Lacan's dislocation psychoanalysis* (M. Levine, Trans.). Cambridge: Cambridge University Press.

Weedon, C. (1987). *Feminist practice and poststructuralist theory.* Oxford: Blackwell.

Werthman, C. (1971). Delinquents in school. In B. R. Cosin et al. (Eds.), *School and society.* London: Routledge and Kegan Paul.

Wex, M. (1979). *Let's take back our space: Female and male body language as a result of patriarchal structures.* Frauenliteraturverlag: Hermine Fees.

Wilshire, D. (1989). The uses of myth, image and the female body in re-visioning knowledge. In A. M. Jagger and S. R. Borno (Eds.), *Gender/body/knowledge: Feminist reconstructions of being and knowing.* New Brunswick, NJ: Rutgers University Press.

Wittig, M. (1969). *Les Guérilleres.* Boston: Beacon.

Woolf, V. (1971). *Orlando.* London: Hogarth Press.

—— (1976). *Moments of being.* London: Triad/Granada.

Zipes, J. (1986). *Don't bet on the prince: Contemporary feminist fairy tales in North America and England.* Aldershot, UK: Gower.

~ Index

~ Permissions

Chapter 1, "The Process of Subjectification." Originally published as B. Davies, "The Subjects of Childhood," in *Shards of Glass: Children Reading and Writing Beyond Gendered Identities* © B. Davies (1993). Reprinted by permission of Hampton Press.

Chapter 2, "The Problem of Desire" © 1990 The Society for the Study of Social Problems. Reprinted from *Social Problems,* Vol. 37, No. 4 by permission of the Society for the Study of Social Problems.

Chapter 3, "The Concept of Agency." Originally published as "The Concept of Agency: A Feminist Poststructuralist Analysis," *Social Analysis,* 30: 42–53 (1991). Reprinted by permission of *Social Analysis.*

Chapter 4, "Women's Subjectivity and Feminist Stories." Originally published in *Investigating Subjectivity,* C. Ellis and M. G. Flaherty (eds.) © 1992. Reprinted by permission of Sage Publications, Inc.

Chapter 5, "Positioning: The Discursive Production of Selves." Originally published in the *Journal for the Theory of Social Behaviour,* 20(1): 43–63 (1990). Reprinted by permission of Blackwell Publishers and Rom Harré.

Chapter 6, "Classroom Competencies and Marginal Positionings." Originally published in *The British Journal of Sociology,* 15(3): 389–408 (1994). Reprinted by permission of *The British Journal of Sociology* and Robyn Hunt.

Chapter 7, "The Subject of Poststructuralism." Originally published as "The Subject of Poststructuralism: A Reply to Alison Jones," *Gender and Education,* Vol. 9, No. 3, pp. 271–282 (1997). Reprinted by permission of Carfax Publishing.

Chapter 8, "Poststructuralist Theory in Practice: Working with 'Behaviorally Disturbed' Children." Originally published in *Qualitative Studies in Education.* Reprinted by permission of Carfax Publishing and Cath Laws.

B. Davies, extracts from *Power, Knowledge, Desire: Changing School Organisation and Management Practice* © 1996 Commonwealth of Australia copyright reproduced by permission.

R. P. McDermott, extracts and figures from *Kids Make Sense: An Ethnographic Account of the Interactional Management Success and Failure in One First Grade Classroom.* Unpublished Ph.D. (1976).

~ About the author

BRONWYN DAVIES is a professor of education at James Cook University in the far north of Australia. Over the last decade she has played a major role in translating the philosophical principles of poststructuralist theory into research practice. Most notable was her best-selling book *Frogs and Snails and Feminist Tales: Preschool Children and Gender,* which has been translated into several languages and received considerable acclaim. Other books include *Life in the Classroom and Playground: The Accounts of Primary School Children, Shards of Glass: Children Reading and Writing Beyond Gendered Identities, Power Knowledge Desire: Changing School Organisation and Management Practice, Poststructuralist Theory and Classroom Practice,* and *(In)scribing Body/Landscape Relations.* Her current work explores the ways in which poststructuralist theory can inform not only the way we ask research questions, but also the way we collect and analyze data. As well, she is particularly fascinated by the processes of writing—how it is we can write differently about what emerges through the research process and also how the act of writing itself is fundamental to that process. Her work seeks to make the principles of poststructuralist theory understandable and usable, and in that process she has made valuable contributions to the body of writing about and within the field of poststructuralist theory.

r a

e bel